King Richard III

ARDEN STUDENT SKILLS: LANGUAGE AND WRITING

Series Editor

Dympna Callaghan, Syracuse University

Published Titles

Antony and Cleopatra, Virginia Mason Vaughn
Hamlet, Dympna Callaghan
Macbeth, Emma Smith
Much Ado About Nothing, Indira Ghose
Othello, Laurie Maguire
Romeo and Juliet, Catherine Belsey
The Tempest, Brinda Charry
Twelfth Night, Frances E. Dolan

Forthcoming Titles

King Lear, Jean Howard
A Midsummer Night's Dream, Heidi Brayman Hackel
The Merchant of Venice, Douglas Lanier

King Richard III

Language and Writing

REBECCA LEMON

Bloomsbury Arden Shakespeare
An imprint of Bloomsbury Publishing Plc

B L O O M S B U R Y
LONDON · OXFORD · NEW YORK · NEW DELHI · SYDNEY

Bloomsbury Arden Shakespeare

An imprint of Bloomsbury Publishing Plc

Imprint previously known as Arden Shakespeare

50 Bedford Square	1385 Broadway
London	New York
WC1B 3DP	NY 10018
UK	USA

www.bloomsbury.com

BLOOMSBURY, THE ARDEN SHAKESPEARE and the Diana logo are trademarks of Bloomsbury Publishing Plc

First published 2018

© Rebecca Lemon, 2018

Rebecca Lemon has asserted her right under the Copyright, Designs and Patents Act, 1988, to be identified as author of this work.

British Library Cataloguing-in-Publication Data
A catalogue record for this book is available from the British Library.

ISBN:	HB:	978-1-474-25335-2
	PB:	978-1-474-25334-5
	ePDF:	978-1-474-25337-6
	eBook:	978-1-474-25336-9

Library of Congress Cataloging-in-Publication Data
A catalog record for this book is available from the Library of Congress.

Series: Arden Student Skills: Language and Writing

Cover design: Irene Martinez Costa
Cover image © The Folger Shakespeare Library

Typeset by RefineCatch Limited, Bungay, Suffolk
Printed and bound in Great Britain

To find out more about our authors and books visit www.bloomsbury.com. Here you will find extracts, author interviews, details of forthcoming events and the option to sign up for our newsletters.

CONTENTS

ACKNOWLEDGMENTS

My engagement with Shakespeare's *King Richard III* is ongoing, and a number of scholars and students have helped sharpen my understanding of the play over the years.

Members of the 2016 Shakespeare Association of America's seminar on "Performing Disability in Early Modern England," and most especially Genevieve Love, shared insights on thinking through and teaching the play's language of deformity.

A World Shakespeare Congress seminar in Stratford-Upon-Avon in 2016 on "Reading Shakespeare Adaptation Historically" provided an occasion to think through the afterlives of *Richard III*; I'm grateful to the seminar members, and especially to its leaders Maurizio Calbi and Deborah Cartmell.

Annaliese Connolly helped initiate my thinking on *Richard III*, and offered astute feedback on my essay for her collection, *Richard III: A Critical Guide*. Two graduate research assistants, Steven Minas and Betsy Sullivan, expertly navigated the range of criticism on the play. Undergraduate research assistants Emma Dyson and David Norton, thanks to USC Dornsife's SHURE program, were able to read through the volume with an eye to its utility for students new to the play.

Graduate students in my seminar on tyranny, and undergraduates in my Shakespeare lecture, helped me to extend and clarify my readings. I'm grateful to members of English 230 for confirming that the readings and assignments I offer in this volume might indeed work for a range of students.

Most of all, I'm grateful to Dympna Callaghan for her guidance through the very enjoyable process of writing this book.

PREFACE

History, Winston Churchill famously claimed, is written by the victors. His adage seems particularly true in the case of the "hunchback" King Richard III. Richard lost the Battle of Bosworth Field to the first Tudor king, Henry VII, and as a result his Tudor enemies wrote the story of his life, condemning him as a twisted murderer and villain. But Richard has arguably had the last laugh. This maligned king has attracted scholarly and popular attention disproportionate to the length of his two-year reign.

The interest in Richard III is especially acute in our generation because he was only laid to rest in 2015, over five hundred years after his death at the Battle of Bosworth. Improbably, his body was discovered in a car park in Leicester, England, thanks to what the *New York Times* and other papers have called "a mind blowing find," "nothing short of miraculous," and "one of the most astonishing archeological hunches in modern history." The body had been thrown unceremoniously into a shallow grave in August 1485, where it remained until a member of the Richard III Society (a twentieth-century society devoted to Richard, promoting a laudatory legacy for the maligned king) had a hunch. Visiting Leicester, Philippa Langley recounts, "I absolutely knew I was walking on his grave," an instinct that was greeted with a degree of disbelief and mockery. But Langley raised funds and eventually brought together a team of archaeologists, engineers, and historians to excavate the ruins of the Greyfriars Priory, located under the modern day car park where Langley had her hunch. Unbelievably, the first cut of the first day produced a skeleton, complete with battle wounds and a curved spine. Genetic testing confirmed the remains to be Richard's.

At long last the notorious hunchbacked king could be given a proper burial. If Franciscan friars disposed of his body hastily in 1485, his 2015 burial attracted thousands of visitors who lined up to see the coffin as it moved through the streets, and lay for three days of viewing in Leicester's cathedral. Then, in a ceremony featuring the Archbishop of Canterbury, a Catholic Cardinal, ten British Army pallbearers, Anglican prelates, the current Richard, Duke of Gloucester, minor royals, famous actors, and a packed audience, Richard III's remains were interred in the cathedral, in a marble tomb near the altar. *The Times* of London called the event "a glorious return for one of history's biggest losers," and the *Daily Mail* railed that a "child killer" was now celebrated. Thus even as his remains are laid to rest, the vexed legacy of Richard continues.

Benedict Cumberbatch, of Sherlock Holmes fame and a distant relative of Richard III, offered a reading at the internment. The poem he read, entitled "Richard" and written by Poet Laureate Carol Ann Duffy for the occasion, features the king's own voice, speaking of his burial:

> My bones, scripted in light, upon cold soil,
> a human braille. My skull, scarred by a crown,
> emptied of history. Describe my soul
> as incense, votive, vanishing; your own
> the same. Grant me the carving of my name.
>
> These relics, bless. Imagine you re-tie
> a broken string and on it thread a cross,
> the symbol severed from me when I died.
> The end of time – an unknown, unfelt loss –
> unless the Resurrection of the Dead . . .
>
> or I once dreamed of this, your future breath
> in prayer for me, lost long, forever found;
> or sensed you from the backstage of my death,
> as kings glimpse shadows on a battleground.

Duffy imagines a Richard with a soul "as incense, votive, vanishing" as the souls of the thousands who visit and view his tomb. Like these visitors, this infamous man faced familiar questions of death and resurrection; but unlike most people his remains reappeared. His resurrection is thus a literal one, as his history continues to unfold in our own age.

Beyond the visitor centers, the car parks, the documentaries, and the reinterment lies another King Richard. And that king is the subject of this volume: Shakespeare's Richard III. Unlike the car park skeleton, this Richard comes down to us as a heap not of bones but of words. Out of these words Shakespeare embeds Richard in a play replete with lush images, complex characters, and a thrilling plot. Written almost entirely in regular verse, without the prose or broken verse that marks later Shakespeare plays, *King Richard III*'s language is at times incantatory, lulling its audience into complacency. This book will help you grapple with those words.

This book begins with an introduction on *Richard III* in Shakespeare's career, considering the historical context of the play. The introduction explores big questions about the play, including its role in the Tudor myth and its representation of Richard's body. The goal here is to expose how even familiar topics invite investigations. Chapter One turns to an intimate study of Shakespeare's language, moving from words to lines to speeches. Our goal: to understand how Shakespeare's words appear in your edition and what range of meanings they open up. Chapter Two studies the play's structure, from its highly textured use of rhetorical form to the prophetic language that forms a counter-discourse in the play. Here we seek to understand how Shakespeare shapes his plot and characters through language. Chapter Three studies the adaptations of the play, particularly as a political allegory on tyranny. This chapter reveals the different applications of the same words, studying how theatre shapes interpretation. Throughout our attention will remain on Shakespeare's most dramatic legacy, his words, with an eye to how we might better understand them. Having accomplished this in the first three chapters, we turn in Chapter Four to your own writing. Here I offer tips and advice as you turn from Shakespeare's pages to your own.

Introduction

King Richard III is one of Shakespeare's most popular plays. This introductory chapter addresses some of the larger issues surrounding this frequently performed, and much debated, play: its theatricality, its potential participation in the Tudor myth of history, and its depiction of Richard's contorted body. In the process we dip our toes into some of Shakespeare's language, before plunging fully into the pool in the volume's main chapters. Our goal for now is to understand how some very familiar chestnuts about the play are less secure, and require more inspection, than one might think. The lesson: read and assess for yourself, take nothing for granted.

King Richard III in historical context

King Richard III is an early play, written in the first third of Shakespeare's career, around 1592 before he was an established dramatist. It is also, as mentioned, one of Shakespeare's most popular. Compelling and theatrical, it is long—and exhausts its primary actor. It is worth considering, what actor would have the talent to play this challenging role? Shakespeare probably considered this same question in shaping the play, and fortunately he had an easy answer: Richard Burbage, the most famous actor of the sixteenth century and, indeed, the first great actor on the English stage. In *Richard III*, Shakespeare wrote the role that made Burbage's career—as well as the careers of other actors in his wake. These famous Richards include the great eighteenth-century actor, playwright, stage manager and producer David Garrick, who played Richard in 1741 to such acclaim that he was taken on as an actor by London's Drury Lane theater; nineteenth-century actor Edmund Kean, famous for his portraits of Shakespeare's villains, among them Richard; mid-twentieth-century actor and founding director of the National Theatre in Britain, Laurence Olivier, whose Richard III appeared at the Old Vic to great acclaim in the 1940s; and Anthony Sher, a principal actor with the Royal Shakespeare Company, where he gained attention as Richard III in 1984.

In taking on the role of Richard, these actors experience—and ride to fame on—the king's particular mixture of infamy and celebrity. The role allows actors to express "an infinite variety of feelings: fear, horror, agony, conflict, interpenetrated with the courage of desperation" (Richmond, 1989, 52), and such variety gives the character, and the actor playing him, a special charisma. Indeed, Shakespeare's Richard has an oddly, and unexpectedly, erotic appeal. One of the few historical anecdotes on Shakespeare speaks precisely to the mix of infamy, celebrity, and eroticism around Richard: a female spectator at one of Burbage's performances of *Richard III* liked him so much in the title role that she asked him to come to her chamber later that evening under the name of the villainous king. But Shakespeare, overhearing her request to Burbage, showed up first—so that when Burbage arrived he was told, in Shakespeare's witty retort (playing on his own name), that William the Conqueror had preceded Richard III. An entry from March 13, 1602 in John Manningham's diary records the incident:

> Upon a time when Burbage played Richard III: there was a Citizen grew so far in liking with him [i.e. a Citizen so attracted to him], that before she went from the play she appointed him to come that night unto her by the name of

Richard III. Shakespeare overhearing their conclusion [i.e. overhearing their agreement] went before, was entertained, and at his game ere Burbage came [i.e. he was already wooing her before Burbage arrived]. Then message being brought that Richard III was at the door, Shakespeare caused return to be made [i.e. replied] that William the Conqueror was before Richard the 3, Shakespeare's name [being] William.

> Mr. [Tous or Curle] /
> (Manningham, [fol. 29v]).

This incident may have been told to Manningham by Mr. Willian Touse, a member of the Inner Temple cited frequently in the diary, or by Edward Curle, Manningham's Middle Temple roommate. The final name is hard to read in the manuscript. Either way, the anecdote is now legendary. It is one of the very few about Shakespeare himself, recorded during his lifetime by a contemporary. And the account speaks not only to Shakespeare's wit, but more centrally for our purposes, to the popularity of Burbage's Richard III. The "him" attracting the "citizen" seems at once the figure of Richard III and Burbage combined.

The play secured the reputation of Burbage and also, not surprisingly, of Shakespeare himself: *Richard III* appeared in multiple quartos during Shakespeare's lifetime, and it is one of the few plays to include Shakespeare's name on the title page. He had written only four or five other plays before this one. By some accounts he had written *Comedy of Errors*, and the three *Henry VI* plays; by other estimates he may have composed the three *Henry VI* plays as well as *The Two Gentlemen of Verona*, *The Taming of the Shrew*, and *Titus Andronicus*. Either way, *Richard III* unquestionably helped secure his reputation as he developed the new medium of the public playhouse for his own uses.

For if Shakespeare was a relatively young writer, the public playhouse itself was also relatively new. The first playhouse was likely opened by James Burbage (father of the actor

Richard Burbage, noted above) in 1576, only fifteen years before this play. And, like any new media, the theater had its share of critics. The mingling of men and women of different ranks in the playhouse, the theater's presence in an allegedly vice-ridden and unregulated area of town known as the Liberties, and the puritan attacks on the theater, all contributed to an atmosphere of transgression that marked the public theater's early years. Our first section will explore this feature of the theater at the time of *Richard III*'s first productions, with an eye to illuminating just how incendiary Shakespeare's play might have been, and might continue to be.

Theater and anti-theatrical prejudices

Shakespeare wrote in a time of social and religious upheaval. The effects of the Reformation were ongoing, with England shifting from a Catholic to Protestant country in the short decades before Shakespeare's rise. Plague, poverty, war, food shortages, and other social crises produced, for some Elizabethan subjects, a sense of a world at its end. Puritan critics were especially dire in their prognostications, warning about the threat of anything from drinking to May games to tobacco. The theater came under special attack, combining as it did entertaining spectacles with sabbatarian threat (i.e. the threat to Christian observance of the Sabbath, as spectators attended the theater rather than church). Thus critic Anthony Munday, in his book called *A Second and Third Blast against Playes and Theatres*, describes theaters as "public enemies to virtue and religion; allurements unto sin; corrupters of good manners; mere brothel houses of Bawdry" (Munday, 1580). Fellow puritan Philip Stubbes, one of the theater's most vociferous critics, concurs. For critics like Munday and Stubbes, plays represent a form of lying: an actor pretends to be someone else, commits sins, and teaches audiences to imitate such vice. Stubbes describes how the theater threatens its audiences by teaching them vices, such as falsehood, fraud (cozenage), deception, hypocrisy, lying, swearing, murdering and more. He writes,

> Whereas, you say, there are good Examples to be learned in them [plays]: Truly so there are: if you will learn falsehood; if you will learn cozenage [fraud]; if you will learn to deceive; if you will learn to play the Hypocrite; to cog [cheat], lie, and falsify; . . . if you will learn to murder, slay, kill, pick, steal, rob and rove [wander]; if you will learn to rebel against Princes, to commit treasons, to consume treasures, to practice idleness . . . If you will learn to play the whoremaster, the glutton, the Drunkard, or incestuous person . . . You need to go to no other school, for all these good Examples may you see painted before your eyes in interludes and plays.
>
> (Stubbes, *Anatomy of Abuses*, 1583, L8v)

Stubbes's laundry list of bad examples—treason, gluttony, incest—indeed resonates with Shakespeare's plays. His characters commit treason, as in *Richard III*, *Macbeth*, and *Hamlet*; his characters are gluttons and drunkards, like Sir Toby Belch of *Twelfth Night* and Falstaff in the *Henriad*. Characters display adulterous and incestuous desire, from Claudius and Gertrude in *Hamlet* through *Antony and Cleopatra* to *The Winter's Tale*. For its critics, the theater stands as a double threat: not only are the actors deemed to be liars, in pretending to be someone they are not (often someone of much higher station, and in much richer clothing); but the actors also perform roles rife with sin. The result is a double imitation, brought to life before thousands of eager spectators who might mimick precisely the errors they see onstage.

One way of approaching Shakespeare's plays is to notice how he responds, implicitly or explicitly, to these critical charges: he thematizes the power of acting and theater in nearly all of his plays, suggesting what can one accomplish with acting, and what we learn through the theater. *Twelfth Night*'s Viola protects herself in Illyria by donning a costume, just as Portia saves the life of Antonio by dressing as a judge in *The Merchant of Venice*. Hamlet ferrets out the truth of Claudius's guilt through a play, just as the Duke discovers vice in Vienna by dressing as a friar in *Measure for Measure*. Paulina tests the fidelity and transformation of Leontes through Hermione's imagined statue in *The Winter's Tale*, while Edgar attempts to mend his father's broken heart through disguise as a beggar at the edge of an imagined cliff in *King Lear*. Theater, Shakespeare's plays reveal again and again, transforms us, answering the critics in his day and asserting the power of the stage for generations to come.

Shakespeare's brilliance in promoting the new theater is on full display in *Richard III*. In choosing early in his career to write about this maligned monarch, he landed on a familiar and popular topic, one arguably designed to appeal to Queen Elizabeth. After all, the story of Richard III ends with the rise of the Tudor house and the ascension of Queen Elizabeth's grandfather, Henry VII, the victor at the Battle of Bosworth Field. The play seems geared to offer a popular and fully approved history lesson to his varied audiences, supporting the monarch and the nation in the process, as the chapter's next section explores. But, as this book will go on to suggest, the play's neat support for the Tudor dynasty is, arguably, compromised by Richard's own theatrical skills—he is the best actor onstage, and his villainy is potentially contagious.

Tudor myth of history

Richard III appears as the fourth and final play in an historical tetralogy (set of four plays) chronicling the Wars of the Roses. *Henry VI*, parts 1, 2, and 3, cover the eruption and continuation of this English civil war fought between the royal houses of Lancaster and York for control of the crown, after the deposition of the Yorkish Richard II by the Lancastrian Henry IV. (Shakespeare chronicles these events later in his career, in his second tetralogy, spanning *Richard II* through the two parts of

Henry IV to *Henry V.*) *Richard III* opens at the moment when the House of York has won the civil war—the reigning King Edward IV, son of the third Duke of York and brother to Richard, has gained the throne, and the Wars seem to be at an end. This is what Richard references in first lines of the play, in a long speech we will study in detail in Chapter One. He opens by saying: "Now is the winter of our discontent / Made glorious summer by this son of York" (i.e. now is the period of civil war over, thanks to the ascension of my brother Edward, Duke of York, to the throne). But Richard's response to this time of peace is hostile: he announces his villainous plans, to set his two brothers in opposition. In fact, we realize, he means to plague the sickly king towards death; to murder his brother Clarence; and to eliminate any other courtiers who stand in his way to the crown.

Despite Richard's reputed villainy, his opponents—in Shakespeare's play, and in historical fact—faced a dilemma. On gaining the throne, Richard III ruled as England's legitimate king. Furthermore, he was a king preoccupied with legal rights. He developed the system of bail that allows prisoners to live outside of prison while awaiting trail. He helped to formulate and enshrine the principle of neutral juries and presumed innocence. His accomplishments at law, and his careful attention to legal procedures in gaining the crown (despite his villainies), created a significant problem for his successor: Henry, Duke of Richmond is, in legal fact, a traitor. He gained the crown by killing Richard, having invaded England from a foreign shore, France. Thus, however legitimate the Tudor house comes to appear historically, its initial ascent to the throne was rocky.

Henry VII's position was further compromised because he did not have a strong claim to the throne. His father, Edmund Tudor, was of Welsh royal lineage with no English claim. It is instead through his mother, Margaret Beaufort, that he traced his royal line: Margaret was the descendant of one of the daughters of John of Gaunt, Duke of Lancaster, born to Gaunt's mistress, Katherine Swynford. John of Gaunt later married Katherine, making her his third wife; and their initially

illegitimate children were later legitimized. But these children—
including Margaret Beaufort's ancestor—were barred from the
succession. Claiming the throne through a problematic
maternal lineage, Henry VII was on the weakest possible
ground in his bid for the crown, although he tried to bolster
this claim through proximity to another royal lineage: his
father was the second husband of the second wife of King
Henry V, a serpentine and even less persuasive claim. So Henry
smartly strengthened his untenable dynastic claims by marrying
someone from the York line, Elizabeth, the only surviving child
of King Edward IV. Henry thus united his Lancastrian line
with her York line, effectively ending the Wars of the Roses,
and silencing dynastic claims from either side.

But since Henry VII's claims were rather weak, and since
England had just endured decades of civil war coming out of
problematic claims to the throne, the new king sought to
secure his reign even further by controlling the historical
record of his rise. Specifically, he commissioned a series of
historians to uphold his right to the throne on spiritual and
ethical grounds, shaping what has become known as the Tudor
myth of history. The myth alleges that Richard III is evil
incarnate, while Richmond (Henry VII) is savior of England,
appointed by God. What might have seemed illegal—invading
the kingdom from abroad and toppling the sitting king—now
appeared the result of divine prompting, healing the nation
and uniting the red and white roses of the royal houses of York
and Lancaster. This myth appears in art, literature and histories
from the period. Henry VII employed painters to shape
portraits of himself and of Richard III, emphasizing his own
open demeanor in contrast to Richard's sidelong glances.
Henry VII also employed an historian by the name of Polydore
Vergil to chronicle his rise. Subsequent historians, including
Thomas More, Raphael Holinshed, and Edmund Hall (as we
will study in more detail in Chapter Two), took up the story. As
did Shakespeare. As one study guide to the play reads, "By
portraying Richard as a hunch-backed villain and Richmond
as a valiant rescuer, Shakespeare validated Queen Elizabeth's

reign, and also created a fictionalized picture of history that has remained through the modern day."

The Richard III Society—the twentieth-century society devoted to restoring the good name of Richard III—is particularly sharp in its critique of the play's role in reinforcing this Tudor-commissioned propaganda. Dedicated to defending the name of Richard, the Society summarizes the myth succinctly, in these terms:

- Richard was a nasty hunchback who plotted and schemed his way to the throne;

- he killed Henry VI's son Edward;

- he killed Henry VI (a sweet, innocent saint);

- he got his brother, the duke of Clarence, executed;

- he killed the Princes in the Tower (sweet, innocent children);

- he killed his wife Anne because he wanted to marry his niece Elizabeth;

- he was a bad king; and so it was lucky that Good King Henry Tudor got rid of him for us.

The Richard III Society challenges this myth on multiple levels, from the tales of Richard's deformity to the horror of interfamilial violence, arguing—for example—that in a time such as the Wars of the Roses, the violent deaths of Henry VI, Edward, Clarence, and even the princes would have been conventional practice.

In assessing Shakespeare's role in perpetuating the Tudor myth, the Society carefully indicates its appreciation for the play as fiction while disputing its truth value, writing: "Many commonly held ideas about Richard III emanate from William Shakespeare's play. The society's view is that Shakespeare's *Richard III* is a wonderful play, with good theater achieved through his villainous character; however it is not history, it does not represent fact." The Society's mission statement provides a useful introduction not only to the historical debates around the Tudor myth itself, but also Shakespeare's role in propagating this myth:

> The Richard III Society may, at first glance, appear to be an extraordinary phenomenon—a society dedicated to reclaiming the reputation of a king of England who died over 500 years ago and who reigned for little more than two years. Richard's infamy over the centuries has been due to the continuing popularity, and the belief in, the picture painted of *Richard III* by William Shakespeare in his play of that name. The validity of this representation of Richard has been queried over the centuries and has now been taken up by the Society.

> The Society is perhaps best summed up by its Patron, the present Richard, Duke of Gloucester: ". . . the purpose—and indeed the strength—of the Richard III Society derives from the belief that the truth is more powerful than lies; a faith that even after all these centuries the truth is important. It is proof of our sense of civilised values that something as esoteric and as fragile as reputation is worth campaigning for."

The mission statement of the Richard III Society lays bare the stakes in reading and interpreting the play for us: does "the picture painted of Richard III by William Shakespeare" constitute "lies" that fly in the face of truth?

On one level, this question has been answered, from an historical perspective at least. The discovery of Richard's body during the Greyfriar's Dig in the Leicester car park in 2012 confirms as true some of the key features of what had seemed a mere myth. First, the remains of Richard's body reveal that he did indeed have a contorted spine; the emphasis on his deformity is not a later addition to the legend, as some scholars have argued. He suffered, archaeologists and scientists found, from an 80-degree pitch of his spine, a significant and painful scoliosis. Thus, the allegations that his frame was twisted or bent are indeed accurate. Second, the number of stab wounds to his corpse, even after death, suggest unpopularity in his own day. This discovery, according to those archeologists and historians who have examined the skeleton, potentially undercuts claims of Richard's broad support among his subjects. Thus Shakespeare might not have invented this villain but rather followed the historical record. RSC actor Jonathan Slinger puts it this way: "What's fascinating is that the dig is changing all that [the notion that Shakespeare's play is propaganda]. Some historians claim Richard wasn't disabled at all, whereas the skeleton suggests that his spine was badly curved ... That wasn't something Shakespeare invented—and so perhaps the play isn't the Tudor propaganda hatchet job that people often assume" ("Richard III: Shakespearean Actors ...", 2013).

But there is another way of approaching the issue of truth and lies in Shakespeare's play—not through the matter of historical record, but through the complexity of the play's language. For arguably we've begun with what should be the end, by studying the play's infamy, rather than its language: we opened by surveying the critics of the theater and historical supporters of Richard. We have yet to dip into Shakespeare's own words, the words that have made Richard himself legendary. For, the play—this volume will suggest in its remaining sections and chapters—leaves us much more aware of Richard's charismatic power, and his claims to our sympathy, than mere propaganda would allow.

One way of challenging the supposition that the play served as a Tudor apology—in shaping Richard's villainy—is through the most obvious and debated aspect of the king, namely his body. The language around his body is some of the most powerful in the play; and the myth or fact of its deformity has fueled debates up to and beyond the moment of the discovery of the historical Richard's remains in a car park in Leicester. This chapter's following sections turn, in our first close investigation into the play's language, to depictions of Richard's body. In doing so, we will carefully examine assessments of Richard's physical frame, with an eye to forming our own views—apart from the Tudor myth of history—about how Shakespeare shapes his famous villain.

Richard III's body

Richard begins the play with a bold pronouncement about his own body. He claims that he is "rudely stamped," "cheated of feature," "deformed," and "unfinished" (1.1.16, 19, 20). And this body justifies, he tells the audience, his exceptional villainy. In his opening soliloquy he chronicles how he is exiled from love-making with a "wanton ambling nymph" (17). He is, he protests, "not shaped for sportive tricks, / Nor made to court an amorous looking-glass" (14–15), he "want[s] love's majesty" (16), and is "curtailed of . . . fair proportion" (18). He thus rejects the role of lover and accepts what he views as his fated position: "I am determined to prove a villain" (30). This role, he reasons, is an inevitable outcome of his frame. And if Shakespeare's Richard opens the play by describing the link between his body and his villainy, other characters agree. In *Henry VI*, Clifford denounces Richard as a "heap of wrath, foul indigested lump, / As crooked in thy manners as thy shape" (*2H6*, 5.1.157–8) and King Henry calls him "an indigested and deformed lump" (*3H6*, 5.6.51). In *Richard III*, Anne calls him a "lump of foul deformity" (1.2.57), and Elizabeth refers to him as "that foul bunch-backed toad" (4.4.81).

In shaping this character, Shakespeare drew on sources that similarly insist upon Richard's link of deformity and villainy. Sir Thomas More is perhaps the most incendiary of these sources, and his lively account of Richard is notorious for its pointed attack. He describes Richard as "little of stature, ill featured of limbs, crooked-backed, his left shoulder much higher than his right, hard-favored in appearance, and such as is in the case of lords called warlike, in other men called otherwise. He was malicious, wrathful, envious, and from before his birth, ever perverse" (More, 1515). Notice how More yokes Richard's physical frame with his character: his body is, he claims, ill, crooked, and hard, as is his spirit. More's characterization influences, in turn, Raphael Holinshed's chronicle account of the king, where he calls him "close and secret, a deep dissembler, lowly of countenance, arrogant of heart" (Holinshed, 1807, 362). He surmises that "the full confluence of these qualities, with the defects of favour and amiable proportion, gave proof to this rule of physiognomy: *Distortum vultum sequitur distorsio morum*" (Holinshed, 1807, 362).

As Holinshed's Latin adage—distorted behavior follows a distorted face—indicates, this imagined connection between Richard's alleged "deformity" and his villainy echoes the views of certain Renaissance physiognomists. The Renaissance was a period when the body supposedly announced one's moral character. Francis Bacon's comments on the link between deformity and villainy in his *Essays* speak to this point. Bacon writes, "Deformed persons are commonly even with nature, for as nature hath done ill by them, so do they by nature; being for the most part (as the Scripture saith) *"void of natural affection;"* and so they have their revenge of nature" (Bacon, 1612, 161). Thomas Hill similarly reasons, "the forms of the members well proportioned, do denote virtue: but evil fashioned, do argue an evil conditioned person" (Hill, 1571, sigs. Ff6v–Ff7). Michael Torrey offers one of the most sustained critical explorations of this link of a distorted body and spirit in relation to *Richard III*, surveying physiognomic literature and writing, "If various bodily traits indicate wickedness and deceitfulness, there can be no more certain sign of evil than deformity. A misaligned body denotes a misaligned soul" (Torrey, 2000, 129). Linda Charnes spells out this link of the body to a range of other meanings: "In early modern England physical deformity was not conceptualized solely in terms of the body. Rather, the 'tricks of Nature' that beset the human frame were articulated as part of a broader set of relationships between and among difference kinds of 'phenomena,' physical and metaphysical. The body was one signifier in an elaborate network of signification" (Charnes, 1993, 22).

This link of deformity and villainy persists in readings of the play. As one student guide to the play notes, "The motivation for his evil deeds throughout the play may have been obvious to Shakespeare's audience: he wanted to exact revenge for his physical deformity. Richard's deformity might also have been viewed as an act of divine retribution for wrongs perpetrated by Richard's ancestors" (First Folio: Teacher Curriculum Guide, Shakespeare Theatre Company). Scholar René Girard puts it this way: "when Shakespeare wrote the play, the king's identity as a 'villain' was well-established. The dramatist goes along with the popular view, especially at the beginning. Richard's deformed body is a mirror for the self-confessed ugliness in his soul" (Girard, 1984, 159). Finally, Allison P. Hobgood comments on precisely this feature of writings on Richard III when she notes, "long after his death and even now in his resurrection, King Richard's body—and the various processes used to diagnose that body—always take center stage. Renaissance writers and historians from Thomas More to Edward Hall, Raphael Holinshed to William Shakespeare obsessed over Richard's physical shape and used it to determine who he was as both a ruler and a man" (Hobgood, 2014, 23). One interesting exercise: survey recent productions of Richard III—either on film, YouTube, or through theater reviews—and note the staging of Richard's body. Some actors play down any deformity, while others augment this aspect of Richard, making the physical performance of the role into a kind of theatrical signature. Here Antony Sher's performance is especially notable. In his book The Year of the King (2006), he chronicles his quest, over many months, to find the proper theatrical expression for Richard's condition, using complex prosthetic devices. He ultimately settled on worn crutches, offering a striking image of spindly legs that evoked, for many reviewers, a spider.

The link of deformity and villainy is so persistent that you might ask: what else can we say—or write, as this is a volume designed to help you write—about it? Richard tells us what to think of his physical frame from the start, after all. Yet despite dramatic stagings and historical assumptions, despite even Richard's self-characterization in the opening speech, it is worth carefully examining the language around Richard's body in the play, to hear whether or not we agree with the assessments that his body is indeed deformed, and that such deformity determines villainy. Does Richard's body really determine his villainy in Shakespeare's rendition of events? Richard tells us, in the opening speech, a resounding yes: "Since I cannot prove a lover . . . I am determined to prove a villain." But the answer is a bit more complicated than even Richard allows, and the status of his body remains an open question, from both an historical and theatrical standpoint. That is precisely why this Arden series concentrates on Shakespeare's language: studying the play's words can offer surprises that might upend even the most familiar—and seemingly evident—truths.

If Shakespeare was allegedly influenced by Tudor propaganda on Richard as a consummate villain, the play's language reveals something unexpected. Shakespeare depicts Richard's frame as much more interpretively rich and transformative than historical record—or even Richard's opening soliloquy on deformity and villainy—allows. As Sharon Snyder writes in her incisive analysis of prejudice and disability, Richard might appear as the "arch-defective in all literature," the pinnacle example of "malevolent disability" (Snyder, 2005, 272). But Richard marshals, as David Houston Wood argues, a dizzying range of narratives to account for his physical capacities:

Richard's achievement in *Richard III*, such as it is, functions politically in situating his deformities at the nexus of the particularities of oppression, in that disability, as it is deployed in the play, signifies against a background that includes classical concepts of the aesthetic (the Beautiful as the Good); medical concepts of pathology (the aberrant as the monstrous); medieval concepts of the marvellous (the fear of the other); a theological tradition that situates disability as a problem requiring the miracle of healing; and in the full range of other stigmatizing traditions that reflect the complexities of non-normative embodiment and selfhood in early modern England.

(Wood, 2013, 130)

Wood's point here illuminates how much meaning Shakespeare packs into Richard's apparent deformity. If this deformity might seem to define and determine him in these various modes—medical, aesthetic, and theological—Richard insists on creating his own stories, his own narratives, out of his body. Perhaps surprisingly, Richard is, in contrast to the theories of Hill and Bacon, not limited but emboldened by his body. He spins tales out of it. He successfully plays a broad range of parts over the course of the drama: battlefield warrior, holy man, lover, beleaguered loyalist, and national ruler, each part seeming to defy or draw upon the disability he argues limits him. As Katherine Schaap Williams writes of the play, "Critics conflate 'disability' with the language of 'deformity,' which Richard himself deploys in the play to describe his distinctive body, and thus fail to distinguish between the plethora of characterizations of his body" (Williams, 2009, para. 2).

Indeed, Richard accomplishes a kind of sorcery with his body. He condemns and thralls Edward's court through references to his frame. To give an example: addressing courtiers in the Council Table scene, Richard seeks to eliminate those who would block his bid to be King. How does he do this? By invoking his own body. Who, he demands, has "prevailed / Upon my body with their hellish charms?" (3.4.60–1). His arm, he cries, is "a blasted sapling withered up" (3.4.68). Richard points to his arm as a sign of witchcraft, allowing him to accuse Hasting's own mistress, the Lady Shore. While Hastings supports Richard, he hesitates to condemn Shore, replying with one word that costs him his life: "if." He says, "If they have done this deed, my noble lord" (72) and

Richard seizes his opportunity: "Talk'st thou to me of ifs? Thou art a traitor. / — Off with his head!" (74–5). My students often puzzle about this scene: "Did we miss something?" they ask. Richard pounces here, and even if we've been prepared for his attack on the unwilling courtier, we're taken aback. This scene reveals Richard's cunning: he uses superstitions, allegations of witchcraft and the devil, to entangle Hastings; and he does it by inventing stories about his own body. Here we see how the play stages, as Williams puts it, "a frenzy of interpretive fervor about what Richard's body really means" (Williams, 2009, para. 1). Is he the victim of witchcraft or merely invoking sorcery to snare a rival? Is his body even "withered" in the manner he claims? These are some of the interpretive questions, rather than firm answers, haunting the play.

The play's audience understands Richard's gestures as mere trickery, but incredibly the onstage audience seems to fall for his lies. This leads to further doubt on the play's easy link of Richard's frame to his villainy: "complicating any simple correlation between Shakespeare's play and physiognomy is the fact that Richard is a successful deceiver" (Torrey, 2000, 126). If his body should announce his villainy (at least according to some of the prejudicial theories of deformity in the early modern period presented above), then why is the court drawn in by him? "Despite," as Torrey argues, "the obvious signs of his wickedness, he repeatedly ensnares his victims . . . In the course of the play, his body alternately does and does not seem to give him away" (Torrey, 2000, 126). Even as Richard insists he is "deformed", then, his physical condition effectively offers him not limitation but freedom: physical, political, and even epistemological freedom. Through his body he is able to play out a range of roles, disarm his opposition, and evade conventions.

Richard is a theatrical shape-shifter in line with Shakespeare's other villains, such as Iago and Edmund, both of whom claim some degree of abuse and alienation; and both of whom use cultural prejudice, fear and hatred to manipulate people.

Indeed, one might argue that Shakespeare develops a character type fully in one play, *Richard III*, compresses this character type into the villainous anti-hero in *Othello*, and then finally stages the character in an even more condensed form, as the subplot's villain in *King Lear*. Thus the energy and inspiration behind a character like Richard III continues to preoccupy Shakespeare much later in his career. For like Iago and Edmund, Richard stages fake scenes, using the theater to make his opponents look guilty when they aren't. Indeed, Richard III— even more than Iago and Edmund after him—is a master of the theater. He dons a number of costumes and roles in the play, and he is the best actor at court. He counterfeits, deceives, plots and pretends, openly acknowleding how acting and theater help him gain the throne. He even serves as a director of sorts, as when he asks Buckingham,

> Come, cousin, canst thou quake and change thy colour,
> Murder thy breath in middle of a word,
> And then again begin, and stop again,
> As if thou wert distraught and mad with terror?

> (3.5.1–4)

Buckingham's reply, "Tut, I can counterfeit the deep tragedian, / Speak, and look back, and pry on every side . . . Ghastly looks / Are at my service, like enforced smiles" (5–9), reinforces the link of acting and villainy asserted by the theater's critics.

If Puritans are worried that acting constitutes a form of lying, Richard provides cold comfort. For Richard revels in theatrical spectacle, even mocking religious piety: "I sigh, and, with a piece of scripture, / Tell them that God bids us do good for evil; / And thus I clothe my naked villainy / With odd old ends, stol'n forth of Holy Writ, / And seem a saint when most I play the devil" (1.3.333–7). Richard's term "play"—he will "play the devil"—seems to indicate a role that he can take on and off: he will play the villain when it suits him, and then he will return to himself, just as an actor takes up a part for a time. Play also means, of course, diversion, playfulness. And this is actually germane for understanding how Richard works. For he seems to embrace scheming. He is having fun, enjoying himself, and this is—we will see—part of his charisma. In the midst of a court besieged by feeble, sick, or grieving characters, Richard is a relief: he's a figure who relishes what's unfolding. Both of these meanings of play—as an acting role, or as enjoyment—seem voluntary: he guides his own path. But as with an actor cast in a role which he must see through to the end, so might we say that Richard has been predetermined to act as a villain, to "play" a villain in the sense of being cast in a role. He is typecast, he is stereotyped, and there is little he can do about it.

This opposition—Richard plays or is forced to play a role—initially seems out of his control: he begins the play lamenting how his body consigns him to a role. Yet we have been teasing out how his body equally offers him a sight for playful manipulation. He deploys it, as we saw above with Hastings, to control the audience, shifting his shape and altering its signification. If Richard uses his "blasted arm" to prove Shore's witchcraft in the Council Table scene, when he assumes power in the second half of the play his frame reveals something else entirely. He and his allies no longer draw attention to his physical difference as a sign of incapacity; they instead reference his body as a sign of his singular fitness for office. Buckingham tells Richard, for example, that in supporting his role as king before the citizens, "Withal, I did infer your lineaments, / Being the right idea of your father, / Both in your form and nobleness of mind" (3.7.12–14). Richard's "form" resembles his father's, Buckingham argues here: he boasts the "lineaments" of the proper king. Buckingham continues to trumpet the rightness of Richard's physical frame later in the scene, arguing before an audience of subjects:

> The noble isle doth want her proper limbs;
> Her face defaced with scars of infamy,
> Her royal stock graft with ignoble plants,
> And almost shouldered in the swallowing gulf

Of dark forgetfulness and deep oblivion;
Which to recure, we heartily solicit
Your gracious self to take on you the charge
And kingly government of this your land.

(3.7.124–31)

Buckingham constructs a binary logic, as Richard so frequently does, between what is the "defaced," infamous and "ignoble," and what is "proper," royal and "gracious." Yet if such oppositions initially signaled Richard's infamous villainy against the proper York ruler, here it indicates the opposite: now Richard has become the gracious royal, against the bad stock of rival claimants. He offers the "proper limbs" England longs for.

This attention to Richard's body climaxes in the scene where he accepts the crown. He appears onstage, called out by Buckingham, and the Lord Mayor, flanked by bishops. The stage direction reads, "*Enter* RICHARD *aloft, between two Bishops*" (3.7.93). Often editors add helpful stage directions, marking entrances and exits that are left unclear in the original sixteenth- and seventeenth-century versions of the play. But in this case, the stage direction appears in all editions. It may not be as famous as *The Winter's Tale*'s "exit, pursued by a bear"— unquestionably Shakespeare's most famous stage direction— but it combines the same effects of horror and humor. The direction creates an immediate visual tableau, as Richard enters from on high, supported by bishops as if he were a divine on earth. In case the tableau isn't striking enough, the Lord Mayor and Buckingham gloss it for us, with the Lord Mayor noting, "See, where his grace stands, 'tween two clergymen!" (3.7.94). Buckingham, too, offers a commentary on what the staged spectacle means: "Two props of virtue for a Christian prince, / To stay him from the fall of vanity; / And see a book of prayer in his hand, / True ornaments to know a holy man" (3.7.95–8). Are these unnamed bishops actors commissioned by Richard, or are they bishops recognized but unnamed by the Lord Mayor, Buckingham and the crowd below? Richard's acting comes to implicate others, as even bishops hover between sincere and counterfeit.

Even more spectacular than transforming bishops to actors, or actors to bishops, is Richard's transformation of his own body: "Cousin of Buckingham, and sage, grave men, / Since you will buckle fortune on my back, / To bear her burden, whe'er I will or no, / I must have patience to endure the load" (3.7.226–9). Here Richard does something at once surprising and compelling—he reframes the physique that he claims held him back at the beginning of the play as the source of his current power. The bent frame he conjured in the opening and in the Council table scene as announcing his villainy and his vulnerability now advertizes his royal status: he is already, even before assuming the crown, bent with the burden of the office. It is as if his body were imprinted with monarchy from the start—what seemed to disqualify him from office now suggests his aptness for it. Drawing attention to his frame at the precise moment of his coronation might surprise us, but it also illuminates the ways in which the oppositions Richard repeatedly invokes are more complex and ambiguous than he claims. Williams argues something like this when she writes, "By presenting his body along a continuum of ability, in which his physical difference becomes more or less apparent depending upon how he emphasizes it, Richard's use of his physical frame—a body that he initially decries—challenges the conceptual binary between able/disabled bodies" (Williams, 2009, para. 3).

We have been studying how the language depicting Richard's body changes over the course of the play. If he begins by calling himself "deformed," he and his allies later draw attention to his "proper lineaments," his back buckled under the "burden" of royal fortune. Shakespeare's Richard thus invokes, only to challenge, the arguments of contemporary physiognomists. As a result, his body invites multiple perceptions and rampant speculations, as most of the play's courtiers—like subsequent historians—debate its status. Furthermore, his body offers a malleable, and largely political, frame that Richard manipulates for a variety of ends. If his frame initially figures his limitations or villainy, it comes to signal royalty, his Yorkist lineage, and boundless service. Thus, the Renaissance historical context—in which difference was perceived as a kind of villainy—does not map neatly onto Shakespeare's play, which instead insists on Richard's interpretive flexibility.

This next section extends this insight into Richard's body further by using the preoccupation with his physical frame as a lens to examine Richard's protean skills more generally. In doing so we find that he distorts, reframes, and redefines a variety of forms, not just his physical one. Richard's body comes to anticipate and indeed figure the *political* and *legal* effects of Richard's exceptional rule: Richard is almost impossible to categorize. Just as his body is and is not a sign of incapacity, so too Richard is and is not a usurper; he is and is not a legitimate king.

Form and deformity in Richard

We have been studying the range of language on Richard's physical frame. He opens the play by suggesting that his body condemns him to the role of villain, but he proceeds to shape-shift and transform his frame in ways that help him to power, whether using his body as a means of condemning others, or pointing to its contours to signal his viability for the crown. In the process the play challenges reductive distinctions between ability and disability, form and deformity. This section shows how we might use this insight on Richard's surprisingly malleable frame to open up questions about form in the play more broadly. For, in his physical claims to exceptionalism, Richard not only *figures* or *represents* deformity (in line with the Tudor myth of history); he also seems to *embrace* what we might call the politics of de-formity. By this I mean he supports a process of dismantling form itself, whether it be the forms of law in marriage rights and state trials, or the forms of faith, in vows and promises. Specifically, Richard's exceptional frame—

whether we call it "deformed" as Richard does, or particularly malleable—figures and indeed justifies his exercise of exceptional political and legal rights. Richard, allegedly inspired by his own body, embraces de-formation in all its lawless possibilities.

Richard's distorted physical form runs in tandem with— and arguably fuels, at least according to Richard himself—his distortion of other forms, be they moral, political, and legal. Marriage, succession, inheritance, and criminal trial: these legal forms are all frustrated by Richard who undermines them for his own purposes:

> It may appear that *Richard III* perfectly enacts the Tudor myth of succession—underneath all the chaos, violence, and betrayal, the sanctuary of succession remains intact as the Tudor reign begins; and yet ... even that principle, that 'form of law,' is compromised in the play ... through Richard's relentless and, in every sense, fruitless assault on ritual and order.
>
> (Carroll, 1992, 204)

Richard makes a mockery of legal procedure, even as other characters repeatedly strain to uphold it. As a result, Richard's exceptionalism seems less a function of his body (despite his own opening justification) and more a feature of his pleasure in suspending laws, codes and conduct upon which other characters and indeed court culture rely.

Richard's legal gestures are mere charades: he tries to persuade the Lord Mayor that the execution of Hastings "against the form of law" was an emergency ("the extreme peril of the case, / The peace of England, and our persons' safety, / Enforced us to this execution" [3.5.44–6]). But we know, as the Scrivener certainly does, that there were no "just proceedings in this case" (67), as the Lord Mayor hopefully puts it. And in fact, Shakespeare goes out of his way to highlight Richard's transgressions of the law, as Jeremy Lopez illuminates in his study of the death of Clarence: "As Edmond Malone points out, Clarence in I.iv speaks as though he has been imprisoned without due process, but 'the truth is, that he was tried and found guilty by his Peers, and a bill of attainder was afterwards passed against him.' The Clarence of the stage struggles against the Clarence of history" (311–12). What is, historically, a death at the hands of Edward IV, Shakespeare reshapes as one prompted by Richard.

Distorting law, Shakespeare's Richard also alters ritual. We can turn to his exchange with Anne, following his opening speech in the play, for an example. Critics have pointed to the wooing scene with Anne as evidence of Richard's charisma. But what has gone less remarked is how, in staging Richard's use of charismatic force to lawless ends, the scene establishes his exceptional sovereignty early on: he makes decisions in the first scene that he carries out in the second and third, exercising power of life and death over other characters. The scene with Anne initiates the chain of encounters in the play that demonstrate Richard's position of superior power outside the law. Here sanctified marriage becomes an inside joke. His ironic invocations of "love" (1.2.192), family and marriage display an earthy realism in contrast to the heavy formality of Anne, who follows an "honourable load," her husband's "hearse" (1.2.1–2). Anne attempts to invoke the law: "Be it lawful that I invocate thy ghost / To hear the lamentations of poor Anne" (8–9). But she demonstrates only the power to curse, a point we will examine at greater length in Chapter Two. Where she might charge Richard, she instead swears at him; where she might indict him juridically, she does so instead emotionally and morally. He is the "devil," a "minister of hell" (45, 46).

As seen in the forged warrant (an indictment for Hastings's arrest that the Scrivener himself questions), as well as the fictive confession and the false wooing, the play creates a joke out of the law. Not only do the characters, such as Clarence, seem misguided or mistaken in their belief in legal procedure, but their faith in law is out of tune with the charismatic force of Richard. The humor, wit, fascination, and villainous power of Richard stand in complete contrast to the bland, tedious, formalistic invocation of law by his opponents. Thus rather than seeing Richard's role as monster and king in opposition to each other, instead we might consider, along with political theorist Giorgio Agamben, how pariah and sovereign can function as reflections of each other. The source of Richard's charismatic power as king comes precisely from his exceptional status as "monster." As Richard says in *Henry VI, Part 3* , "I am myself alone" (5.5.83). He has "no brother," and is like "no brother" (80). Finally, he fails to understand "love," a feeling "resident in men like one another" (82), but not in him. He is the exception to the rule of love, family, and fellow feeling.

We will return to the issue of Richard's exceptionalism in Chapter Two. For now, we might end our analysis of Richard's form by acknowledging its theatricality. Indeed, he ushers in a state of Shakespearean characterization that flourishes through the dramatist's career. A consummate actor, Richard began the play able to transform himself through imaginative feats. He boasts of this: "I can add colors to the chameleon / Change shapes with Proteus for advantages / And set the murderous Machevil to school" (*3 Henry IV*, 3.2.16). Richard's famous changeability, in adopting so many roles with such charismatic and successful vigor, anticipates the metatheatrical characters that fill Shakespeare's stage, and the actors who bring them to life. Think of the Shakespearean shape changers after him, from Viola to Ariel, Hamlet to Iachimo. For actors in Shakespeare's day attempted to practice precisely the exceptionalism that Richard embodies, reshaping themselves for the number of roles they adopt onstage. Just as Richard moves his frame with different environments, so too with actors, who reshape themselves for each part, and for the variations within that part. An early modern actor was deemed capable of changing not merely his speech and costume but also, as Joseph Roach brilliantly explores, his humorological body—namely, the body that was, according to early modern medical theory, governed by four humors that controlled human mood and health. Actors were capable of "precisely

controlling the instantaneous transitions between passions"
(Roach, 1985, 42), manipulating their bodies for theatrical
effect. Figures like Edward Alleyn and Richard Burbage, who
played Richard III, were famous for their ability to shape-
shift on stage. Exhibiting "Ovidian alterations of bodily
state," these players demonstrated a range of passions through
manipulation of their humors, a practice that allowed
transformations from role to role, and at different moments
within a single role. As Thomas Heywood writes of Alleyn, in
lines that could easily stand for Richard III, he is a "Proteus
for shapes, and Roscius for a tonge / So could he speak, so
vary" (Roach, 1985, 41–2).

It is this protean nature of Shakespeare's art that we will
continue to explore in the chapters that follow, investigating
how, in *Richard III*, words, lines, speeches and characters
transform before us, producing kaleidoscopic effects. How
does Shakespeare use language, in all its variety of forms, to
shape and shift his characters? This chapter explored one
angle on such linguistic variety, studying the contradictory
evocations of Richard himself. We will take up these questions
in subsequent chapters, exploring key words, sentences, and
speeches, as well as the play's dynamic structure, and finally its
various adaptations. For now, this chapter's last section turns
to the critical conversations on this play to help give you a
sense of the range of readings coming out of one notoriously
variable character and the play that contains him.

King Richard III in criticism

Most Shakespeare plays have attracted a daunting amount of
critical attention, and *Richard III* is no exception. Like other
writers in this *Arden: Language and Writing* series, I encourage
you to draw on your own close engagement with the words of
the play in writing about Shakespeare. Build up from there to
create your hypotheses and arguments, before turning to some
of the play's critical debates. If you start with criticism you risk

losing your own insights and voice. I promise there are original and fresh arguments to be made about Shakespeare, but you are much more likely to discover those in the text itself. Criticism is at its most helpful when it allows you to bolster and nuance, as well as reassess, challenge, and strengthen or rethink, the argument you've begun to form through your own careful reading of the play. With that caveat in mind, this section offers a brief introduction to some of the critical debates surrounding the play. Much criticism concentrates on two issues: the play's status as and in history; and the main character's theatrical body.

In examining the play as and in history, a range of critics have asked questions about the type of history it stages: does the play participate in the Tudor myth of history, offering a form of providential history (with providential history being the view that God controls human history and provides continual guidance in its unfolding)? Or, by contrast, is the play challenging such providential readings by depicting Richard's charisma and insisting upon his individual ambition? This is a debate that has flourished since the work of early twentieth-century critic E. M. W. Tillyard. To understand such debates on the play in and as history, Martine Van Elk's essay, cited in this volume's bibliography, proves especially helpful. She illuminates how "we can see this play as not simply presenting a providential or secular reading of history and identity, but as being *about* the struggle between these views" (Van Elk, 2007, 12–13). That is to say, the play is not just about God's plan unfolding in the ascension of the Tudor Henry VII at the end (the providential view), nor is it about a human and secular power struggle between two ambitious men (the secular view). Phyllis Rackin also summarizes the issues well when she notes the "gradual separation of history from theology" in the play, as "explanations of events in terms of their first cause in divine providence" give way to "the effects of political situations and the impact of human will and capabilities" (Rackin, 1990, 6). The play stages, in other words, the emergence of the modern, secular, individualistic view of history over the medieval, God-centered, providential world view, based in theology.

Critics have also challenged Shakespeare's role in upholding the Tudor myth. For Marjorie Garber (1987), the play speaks to the distortions of history itself, serving as an allegory for what happens to the historical record as it is adapted, altered and revised to support the ideological claims of those in power. Mark Thornton Burnett (2002) and William C. Carroll (1992) both explore fears about England's political future, Burnett by reading Richard's monstrosity as a figure for England's historical insecurity, and Carroll by exploring how Richard's careful manner of succeeding to the crown undercuts the process of succession more broadly: the play's ascending monarch, Richmond, gains the throne through illegal means, but with ethical and popular support.

Critics also assess the play in relation to debates about the nature of tyranny in Elizabethan England. Rebecca Bushnell (1990) explores Richard through the lens of tyranny, while playing particular attention to his sexual and political desires in gaining the throne, as he deploys seduction in various forms to secure his rule; Joel Elliot Slotkin (2007) offers a complementary reading, teasing out the link of villainy to sexual attraction, analyzing how Richard's villainy and deformity serve as erotic draws for both characters and audience. He points to the wooing scene with Anne for evidence, since here Richard does not make her forget his villainy; he in fact reminds her of it. More directly related to issues of tyranny, Nick Myers (1999) offers a precise engagement with the legal definitions of the tyrant, Morton J. Frisch (1993) provides a more character-criticism-based approach, Rebecca Lemon (2013) explores Richard's tyranny in relation to contemporary political philosophy on the exceptional ruler, and Rob Carson (2013) studies related questions about the play's relationship to resistance theory flourishing at the time of the play's initial publication.

Critical debates about Richard's theatrical body take several approaches. First critics assess the relationship, explored above, between his body and his identity. Michael Torrey (2000) surveys the literature on how Richard's body betrays his crooked soul, and in the process complicates the easy parallel between deformity outside signaling deformity within. On the connection of body to identity, Janet Adelman's reading of Richard, as turning to theater because of his own isolation and emptiness, proves especially helpful:

> Richard empties himself out in *Richard III*, doing away with selfhood and its nightmare origins and remaking himself in the shape of the perfect actor who has no being except in the roles he plays. . . . [It is] a defensive response to his fear that his shape and his selfhood had been given him, fixed by his deformation in his mother's womb.
>
> (Adelman, 1992, 8–9)

Katharine Maus explores interiority in the play as well, helping us to see some of the complexity at the heart of Shakespeare's characters generally, as they exhibit two alternating theories of the self: "one, that selves are obscure, hidden, ineffable; the other, that they are fully manifest or capable of being made fully manifest. These seem to be contradictory notions, but again and again they are voiced together, so that they seem less self-canceling than symbiotically related or mutually constitutive" (Maus, 1995, 28–9). The difference between an unexpressed interior and a theatricalized exterior appears acutely in the case of Richard III, who manipulates the roles of known theatrical villains, such as the Vice and Machiavel. Robert Weimann and Douglas Bruster (2008) also explore Richard's theatricality in their study of the Vice in mid-Elizabethan morality plays.

In addition to the link of theater and the body, critics investigate the play's sizeable and notably variable language on monstrosity. Linda Charnes's (1993) reading of Richard in relation to notoriety—especially his notorious body—has proved critically generative, influencing a range of subsequent readings of monstrosity in the play. Mark Thornton Burnett offers one of the most extended discussions, writing that "'Monstrosity' is invoked in numerous senses, and Richard himself constitutes a confusing amalgam of single and multiple 'monstrous' features. Nor is Richard ever described as a 'monster': he is simply a composite of 'monstrous' markers and behaviours. This is an index, perhaps, of what happens to a discourse when politics appropriates it to meet a representational imperative" (Burnett, 2002, 93). Bethany Packard (2013) explores how Richard appropriates the narrative of his birth for political purposes, deploying his physical deformities—particularly the story of his baby teeth—as rhetorical devices to justify his ruthless and deceitful stratagems. Finally, Ian Frederick Moulton examines the language of monstrosity in the play next to ideas about masculinity, arguing that Richard functions as "both a critique and an ambivalent celebration of excessive and unruly masculinity and, in doing so, highlights the incoherence of masculinity as a concept in early modern English culture" (Moulton, 1996, 255).

In exploring Richard's theatrical body, critics have also begun to analyze Richard in relation to evolving critical assessments on early modern disability. The foundational work of David Mitchell and Sharon Snyder (2006) on narrative prosthesis and disability helps to initiate this rich discussion of Richard and disability since, as Mitchell and Snyder point out, Richard is one of three figures that "continually surface as evidence" for the notion of disability as "a restrictive pattern of characterization that usually sacrificed the humanity of protagonists and villains alike" (Mitchell and Snyder, 2000, 17). Katherine Schaap Williams's work on Shakespeare and disability offers an illuminating reading of the play. It "remains ambiguous" about his body, she argues, "staging instead a frenzy of interpretive fervor about what Richard's body really means" (Williams, 2009, para. 1). Marcela Kostihova, too, suggests that Shakespeare is "surprisingly ambiguous in describing the physical nature of Richard's deformity" and "this ambivalence challenges each production to invent its own bodily projection of Richard's evil interiority" (Kostihova, 2013, 136; see also Hobgood, 2014). Finally, Vin Nardizzi illuminates Richard as "a powerful source of genealogical disablement" within his family who nonetheless serves as a crutch to prop up the kingdom (Nardizzi, 2016, 66).

This survey of critical debates helps you get your toes wet. I invite you to investigate the continually growing bibliography of articles and books on the play. But I'll end this chapter by noting one more arena for investigation: on the adaptations and afterlives of *Richard III*, in the theater and performance. Here, Anthony Sher's diary of his role as Richard III in *The Year of the King* is a highly original and compelling contribution. The works of Graham Holderness (2006, 2007, 2013) and Margaret Litvin (2007) on Arab world adaptations of the play are insightful; as is the work of Jim Casey (2009), Scott Colley (1992), and Hugh Richmond (1989) on *Richard III* productions on stage and screen. Gillian Day's (2002) volume for Arden Shakespeare offers a survey of Stratford productions of the play in the second half of the twentieth century; and the interviews with actors in the *Players of Shakespeare* series are illuminating (Jackson and Smallwood, 1994; Smallwood, 1998, 2004). Finally, Philip Schwyzer (2013) offers a book-length study of the afterlives of Richard III by tracing the remains of the king as they appear in material artefacts and buildings, popular traditions, textual records, and administrative and religious institutions and practices— and in doing so he investigates the role of Shakespeare's play in preserving this Richardian legacy.

Writing matters

This chapter has invited you to interrogate the evidence before you, particularly when it comes to truisms on the play, such as its status as propaganda, or such as the condition of Richard's body. I thus offer suggested topics that rely on similar skills of observation and analysis. First I ask you to think about the kind of political and prejudicial work that is being done (or undone) in the range of animal images in the play. Introducing you to some of the debates about the early modern theater, this chapter has also surveyed some of Richard's tactics as an actor himself. The second prompt below invites you to explore his theatricality further.

Images

Think about the imagery of animality and animals in the play, from Richard's heraldic image of the boar to the animals in Margaret's prophecy. Why is there such a persistent association of Richard with animals? What kind of animals?

Richard is frequently compared to animals, but these references vary widely: he is called, among other things, a toad, a dog, a hog, a spider and a boar. Why is there such persistent animal imagery? How might these characterizations of Richard differ from one another? Here you might choose to focus on one image (the boar, for example); or you might focus on one set of images (carnivorous animals); or you might choose to compare different images (toad, spider, boar); or you might want to examine how Richard uses animal imagery to describe himself (why would he do this?). The challenge is just figuring out *your analysis of how these animal images operate*, rather than summarizing the scenes with animals and offering a big statement (Richard isn't human, he's an animal: this isn't an analytical point). You might consider, are there any beneficial or elevated animals? *Or* are animals always perceived as lower than humans? What might this mean? One way into the topic might be thinking about staging. Antony Sher was inspired by the animal imagery in conceiving of his Richard: he tells his director, "'we play him as a four-legged creature.' In the text there are many animal references—boar, hog, toad, spider, hedgehog, and best of all . . . 'Hell-hound'" (Sher, 2006, 118).

Theater

Trace the different roles Richard adopts, shaping an argument about the effects of using theater within the play itself.

Richard plays the villain, the devoted brother, the ardent wooer, the pious Christian, and loving uncle. How does Richard's vocabulary and syntax vary, depending on his roles? What does the play expose about the power of language and acting, in staging this range of roles for one character? Is Richard the only character who uses theatrical tricks, or do any admirable characters also feign and counterfeit? If it is only Richard, what might that suggest about Shakespeare's relationship to his own art: what might his play reveal about the power of theater itself? You might also consider Richard's talent with language against the skills or limitations of other characters: does Richard's skill with language draw linguistic felicity into question, given that he's a villain?

CHAPTER ONE

Language in Print:
Words, Lines, Speeches

What text is this?

Who decides what words appear in the Shakespeare edition you are reading? Is it Shakespeare? Yes. And no. The purpose of this chapter is to help introduce you to the words in your copy of *King Richard III*. We will do this in two ways. First, we will discuss the publication of Shakespeare's play, in its various editions printed during his lifetime and after his death. Then we turn to variations between these editions: in spelling, punctuation, additions and omissions. Having laid the groundwork for understanding how the printed play appears before us, we can then dive into the words on the page, paying special attention to the play's famous and lengthy opening speech. This requires study of Richard's skilled use of rhetorical forms to win over his audience, on and off stage. *Richard III* is, after all, one of Shakespeare's most rhetorically self-conscious plays. As Russ McDonald puts it, "the surface of the text repeatedly and proudly calls attention to itself" (McDonald, 1989, 466). We also examine Richard's use of theatrical spectacle, as he moves from playing the victim to the villain, and many roles in between. Throughout, our attention will remain on the play's language at the level of individual words (such as "now"), specific lines ("I am determined to prove a villain"), and key speeches ("Now is the winter of our discontent") in order to introduce you to the most important building blocks in approaching this and any Shakespeare play.

King Richard III in print: Quartos and folios

Richard III was one of Shakespeare's most popular plays. It was reprinted frequently, in many editions. Just to give you a sense of how popular it was, the play appears in eight quarto editions (1597, 1598, 1602, 1605, 1612, 1622, 1629, and 1634), and four folio editions (1623, 1632, 1663, and 1685). Some context is required to highlight the significance of this information: a quarto edition is a pamphlet comprised of full sheets of paper folded twice, to produce four leaves; with print on the front and back sides, each full sheet of paper in a quarto produces eight pages of text. By contrast a folio edition is a much larger book in which the full sheets of paper are folded only one time, resulting in two pages; with printing on the front and back sides, a full sheet of paper in a folio yields four pages of text. For *Richard III* to have eight different quarto editions, and four folio editions, speaks to its startling popularity with buyers of both cheaper and more expensive books. By contrast we might think of the eighteen Shakespeare plays that appeared for the first time only in the 1623 First Folio, from *Comedy of Errors* through *The Tempest*. Given the number of editions of *Richard III*, we might consider Lukas Erne's point about Shakespeare's involvement in—and reliance upon—the book trade in establishing his reputation. Against those who assume Shakespeare had no interest in publishing his works, Erne writes that Shakespeare "anticipated a readership for his plays, and, being in an economically privileged position as company (and later playhouse) shareholder, he could afford to write longer play texts than he knew would be performed, in the knowledge that the full texts would be published and read" (Erne, 2013, 10). Erne's last point, on "longer play texts," is particularly germane for *Richard III*: when printed in 1597, in the edition now known as the first quarto (Q1), it was likely the longest play ever printed in English.

The sheer number of editions (eight quarto editions, Q1–8, namely the smaller, cheaper volume, and four folio editions, F–F4, namely the expensive, large volume) might signal an editorial nightmare, given the potential for textual variants (as a result of printer error, or authorial revision, or alternate source texts). In the case of plays like *King Lear* and *Hamlet*, for example, the significant differences between quarto and folio editions necessitates either parallel text publications (i.e. treating the editions as separate but related plays), or significant labor in combining the disparate texts. In the case of *Richard III*, textual variations between these twelve versions do pose some challenges, and we will take up some of those challenges later in this section. To give one example here: scholars previously imagined the first quarto of the play to be a memorial reconstruction, based on a missing prompt book (a memorial reconstruction being the transcription, or re-construction, of the play from an actor's memory). As W. W. Greg wrote in his defense of this theory, the quarto editions are of too poor quality to be anything other than a botched reconstruction by someone other than Shakespeare; furthermore, Greg argues, the embarrassing first quarto is unrelated to the later, high-quality Folio: "To suppose that Shakespeare, or for that matter any competent writer, could have written the quarto text as it stands, seems to me out of the question; given the quarto text, to suppose that the Folio was produced by a process of revision, mere fatuity [foolishness]" (Greg, 1938, as cited in Maguire, 1996, 362). But more recent scholars have challenged this theory of memorial reconstruction, based on careful comparisons of texts; and they have instead argued—in defiance of Greg's argument— that the first quarto is indeed a draft, later revised for the Folio (see Maguire, 1986, 299–300; Urkowitz, 1986, 466).

Although such debates are important for Shakespeare scholars in understanding the range of texts before us, the differences between these versions of *Richard III* are nowhere near as significant as with plays like *Hamlet* and *King Lear*, not least because the quarto and folio versions of the play are both printed from good manuscripts. As the Arden editor of the play, James Siemon, writes,

> Q1 [First Quarto] was printed from a high-quality manuscript (QMS) of uncertain nature provided by Shakespeare's acting company, the Lord Chamberlain's Men. Twenty-six years later, F [First Folio] was printed from copy that incorporated at least one (Q3, 1602) and probably more than one of the quartos derived from Q1 (Q3, and Q6, 1622), along with accumulated printing errors, while also referring to another, different but highly authoritative manuscript (FMS).
>
> (Siemon, 2009, 417)

Because both the quarto and folio editions come from authoritative sources—Shakespeare's own playing company, and the Folio editors connected to this playing company—we avoid some of the conundrums arising with the publication of a properly "bad" or challenging quarto, like Q1 of *Hamlet*. Instead, even in an era in which editors have moved away from producing conflated texts (i.e. combining various versions of the play into one editorially created text), editions of *Richard III* tend to combine portions of the folio and quarto versions, a task made simpler by the fact that the versions are identical for a good portion of the play (3.1.1 to 3.1.166, and from 5.3.49 to the end of the play) (Siemon, 2009, 419). The portions of the play that differ are nonetheless enough in accordance that, as Siemon reminds us, "E. K. Chambers could claim, with only slight exaggeration, that 'in the main the texts agree in arrangement, speech for speech, and even line for line'" (Siemon, 2009, 419).

There are still some interesting differences we should consider as we begin to approach the play, however. First, the Q1 (1597) title page for *Richard III* reads "As it hath been lately Acted by the Right honourable the Lord Chamber-laine his servants." The quarto reprint the following year, 1598, adds "*By* William Shake-speare" to the title page. Very few title pages list the playwright in the first place; to add a playwright's name to the title page *after* the play had been published anonymously was unparalleled. As Erne tells us, "for an anonymously published play to be ascribed to a playwright in a later edition was an extremely rare phenomenon ... Most title pages slavishly followed that of the preceding edition" (Erne, 2003, 82). He singles out three Shakespeare plays as exceptions: "Apart from *Richard II*, *Richard III*, and *1 Henry IV*, there are hardly any exceptions—and none during Shakespeare's lifetime, as far as I am aware—to the rule that once a play had been published anonymously, it remained so in the following editions" (Erne, 2003, 58). For Erne, the publication of subsequent quarto editions of *Richard III* with Shakespeare's name, after the publication of the first quarto and during Shakespeare's lifetime, suggests the author's involvement in the printing trade, and his concern to build up his own reputation through publication. The fact that *Richard III* is one of only three plays to which Shakespeare added his name might well indicate not only the play's popularity, but also his unusual desire to claim authorship for it.

Another aspect of the play's printing history worth considering is the location of are *Richard III* in the first Folio. Quarto editions are single prints of the plays. But the Folio edition contains nearly all of Shakespeare's plays. How would you arrange them, if it were up to you? By the date of composition, from Shakespeare's first play to his last? By genre, and then in chronological order within each genre (i.e. the Comedy section would begin with his earliest comedy and end with his last)? If you choose either of these very logical methods for arranging his plays, you would differ from the compilers of the first Folio. Arranging the plays within the generic

subheadings of Comedies, Tragedies, and Histories, the Folio
does not then list the history plays by date of composition, as
we might expect, from the first history play Shakespeare wrote
(*Henry VI*) to the last. Instead the Folio arranges the history
plays chronologically according to subject matter, listing "The
Life and Death of Richard the Third" as the penultimate
history, followed by "The Life of King Henry the Eight." Yet
Richard III was one of the first histories Shakespeare composed.
The Folio's arrangement of plays in historical order, not in
order of composition, might seem logical in its own way, but it
is worth noting its effect: the editors imply, in the very
arrangement of plays, that Shakespeare is shaping the history
of England, from the reign of Richard II through the Wars of
the Roses to the ascension of Henry VIII. The editors might
even be suggesting we read these plays in turn, as an extended
story. It is just that, as in the case of the Star Wars cycle, these
plays were not written or produced in chronological order:
Shakespeare started in the middle and worked his way back to
the beginning.

Another noteworthy difference between the Folio and
previous quartos: while the Folio lists *Richard III* as one of the
final history plays, and the header for the play reads "The Life
and Death of Richard the Third" on its printed pages, the Folio
also advertises the play as a tragedy. The play's title page reads
"The Tragedy of Richard the Third: with the Landing of Earl
of Richmond, and the Battle at Bosworth Field." For our
purposes, this shift of genre proves one of the most interesting
variations between all of the texts of *Richard III*. Deemed a
history play in the Folio, *Richard III* is also called a "tragedy"
there, as well as in one of the quarto editions. Thus Q1 of 1597
reads, on its title page, "THE TRAGEDY OF King Richard
the third. Containing, His treacherous Plots against his brother
Clarence: the pitiful murder of his innocent nephews: his
tyrannical usurpation: with the whole course of his detested
life, and most deserved death." This shift of genre—from
tragedy to history to tragedy again—and of detail, from the
death of Clarence and the nephews in the quarto, to the landing

of Richmond and the battle in the Folio—could be taken to reveal shifting interests in the play. The quarto emphasizes the tragic deaths of Richard's family, including the children; the Folio edition draws attention instead to the rise of Henry VII, and the historical battle at Bosworth Field. If the Folio edition is also a tragedy, it is worth asking, for whom? Not for Richmond, clearly. For England? For the king himself? For the courtiers he murdered?

Thus questions about printing and editing bring us to issues of genre, as we meditate on Richard III as a potentially tragic character. Richard does not fit the mold of Aristotelian tragedy, insofar as Aristotle requires a tragic hero be a good person with a decent, if imperfect, character (one of the writing prompts for this chapter asks you to consider Shakespeare's play in relation to classical theories of tragedy). Richard does, however, accord with another model of tragedy: the medieval model, charting the fall of great humans in manner of Giovanni Boccaccio's *De Casibus Vivorum Illustrium*, a particularly popular text in the early modern period. Comprising fifty-six biographies of famous historical figures who flourish and then fall, Boccaccio's *De Casibus* started with the biblical Adam and continued through figures like Trojan King Priam, Samson, Dido, Alexander the Great, Antony and Cleopatra, and Caesar to King Arthur. Influential for English authors from Chaucer through the anonymous *Mirror for Magistrates*, the *de casibus* form of tragedy became popular onstage through Christopher Marlowe's larger-than-life heroes, such as shepherd-turned-emperor Tamburlaine, who conquers central Asia, or the famous necromancer Doctor Faustus. Shakespeare followed this model in crafting *Richard III*, tracing Richard's sharp rise and precipitous fall.

Yet questions about precisely how this play functions as tragedy remain, and our answers influence interpretive choices in reading the play. The play, most obviously, is funny: so funny that it presents a challenge for the actor who is also aware of its tragic genre. This was the case for actor Antony Sher as he prepared for his celebrated 1984 rendition of Richard onstage with the Royal Shakespeare Company. He recounts, "We [he and Adrian Noble, an assistant director at the RSC] talk about *Richard III* and I mention my worry about the humour in the play—I'm finding it increasingly funny each time I read it—in terms of it being a tragedy" (Sher, 2006, 149). Like Sher, we might worry about this discontinuity: is the play a tragedy, a history, or even, potentially, a comedy? We will return to these questions later in the chapter.

Editing the quartos and First Folio

For now, let's turn to some examples of variations between the printed texts and consider how they might impact how we read. The copy of *Richard III* you are reading is the result of editorial effort to bring the most authoritative text of the play to you. But this is not a straightforward process. The gold standard of Shakespeare texts is in many respects the First Folio of 1623 that we discussed above. This was a monumental publication, and remains the definitive edition for most of the plays. But in the case of *Richard III*, the Folio edition altered a play that had been in print for twenty-six years, in eight editions (Q1–8). So alterations that appear in the Folio need to be considered with care even if, as suggested above, these differences are nowhere near as impactful as they are for some other Shakespeare plays. In this section, we consider a variety of such differences, to help give you a sense of precisely what it means to analyze Shakespeare's language, from the individual speeches, to the words, to the punctuation.

At the level of the speeches, we might begin by considering how the Folio edition adds new passages. One such passage is 4.4.288–342, included in the Folio and modern editions but not in the quarto. It is, arguably, a key passage. In the scene, Richard and Queen Elizabeth spar as he attempts to woo her daughter. Richard echoes—in the lines absent from earlier quartos—his earlier wooing of Anne, claiming that he killed Elizabeth's family because of his love for her: "Say that I did all this for love of her" (4.4.288), he tells her mother, as he had told Anne: "'twas thy beauty that provoked me . . . 'twas thy heavenly face that set me on" (1.2.183–5). Just as he claimed to kill Anne's husband to grant her a better husband, he tells the queen, "If I did take the kingdom from your sons, / To make amends, I'll give it to your daughter" (4.4.294–5). As the audience, we've heard this logic before—and we know it is false. What do we make of this repetition in the Folio edition? What difference does it make, to have these additional lines in the play? This is where your work as a careful reader of Shakespeare's language comes in. To my ears, this repetition on Richard's part makes him seem sloppy, and fits nicely with the other missteps that Richard makes at this late point in the play. If his argument worked with Anne, a grief-stricken woman who is politically isolated and whom he woos directly, it is less likely to work with a mother whose children he just murdered. Furthermore, if Richard could sustain his bid for Anne by claiming he loved her, in this later scene Richard mixes his brief claim of love with more obviously political arguments on the benefit of this marriage. Even Richard, it seems, cannot sustain the masquerade of his love for Elizabeth. What we might get out of this speech, probably included in your edition of the play but absent from all editions in Shakespeare's lifetime, is an increased emphasis on Richard's fall: we've watched him juggle his various plots successfully, but on gaining the throne he—like the Macbeths after him—lets preoccupation with the insecurity of his rule overwhelm him. He oversteps himself, and this speech is one place we see this.

Because of this additional material in the Folio, editors believe that the compilers of the Folio had access to a manuscript version, now lost, which they call Folio Manuscript (FMS). Lest we begin to think that the Folio is therefore the definitive text, however, it is worth noting that the Folio also excludes material from the quarto edition, including 4.2.97–114, the scene in which Richard ignores Buckingham as he requests the earldom he had been promised. Specifically, the Folio misses out on one of Richard's wittiest images:

Buckingham as a clock jack, striking the hour in the repetition of his request for the earldom: "like a jack, thou keep'st the stroke / Betwixt thy begging and my meditation" (4.2.112–13). What I find especially clever about this image is its invocation of Buckingham as an unthinking automaton, an automated clock part that fulfills his duties mindlessly. Richard not only refuses Buckingham, then, but he humiliates him for bringing up the dukedom in the first place. The implication, to push on this image a bit further, is that Buckingham's moment of independent thought—pausing to consider the murder of the nephews—infuriated, but also possibly impressed, Richard. Now that Buckingham comes slinking back, wanting compensation, Richard mocks him as a mechanical device, an entirely predictable, inhuman tool.

Reading Shakespeare's language, as these Folio and quarto excerpts reveal, involves establishing precisely what his language is—and what difference it makes, to include or exclude passages from the play. It's not that you need to comb through all quarto and folio editions of the play to establish your own master text. But it is more a question of noticing, as you read, what effect certain speeches and images have on your understanding of characters and plots.

Typesetting

Another key difference in printed versions of the play, beyond cuts and inclusions, lies in punctuation, spelling and capitalization. To give an example, let's turn to the opening speech. Here are the first lines of the play in the Folio edition:

Now is the Winter of our Discontent,
Made glorious Summer by this Son of Yorke:
And all the clouds that lowr'd upon our house
In the deepe bosome of the Ocean buried.
Now are our browes bound with Victorious Wreathes
Our brused armes hung up for Monuments;

Our sterne Alarums chang'd to merry Meetings;
Our dreadfull Marches, to delightfull Measures.
Grim-visag'd Warre, hath smooth'd his wrinkled Front:

And here are the opening lines from the Arden edition:

Now is the winter of our discontent
Made glorious summer by this son of York,
And all the clouds that loured upon our house
In the deep bosom of the ocean buried.
Now are our brows bound with victorious wreaths,
Our bruised arms hung up for monuments,
Our stern alarums changed to merry meetings,
Our dreadful marches to delightful measures.
Grim-visaged War, hath smoothed his wrinkled front;

The most obvious difference lies in the use of capitalization. One effect of the Folio's more generous use of capitals is to suggest a kind of allegorical or symbolic power to some of the references: Ocean might appear a mythological figure, for example, such as Neptune; and the oppositions between Alarums and Meetings, Marches and Measures appear more starkly. The capitalization might be taken, as one actor of Shakespeare suggests, to show the key words. Richard Cordery, who played Buckingham in Michael Boyd's production of *Richard III* at the Swan Theatre in 2001, puts it this way: an "aspect of the First Folio to which I attach huge importance is the capitalization of words ... It seems to me that the work has been done for the actor here. I am not advocating the 'emphasizing' of the capitalized words. Rather one selects those words with initial capital letters as the vital weigh-stations on the route through the speech" (Cordery, 2004, 189). Thus for Cordery, who follows the Folio edition of the plays as he prepares for the stage, this speech is a treasure trove of such "weigh-stations," key punctuated moments.

In the Arden edition, by contrast, the capitalization of War alone draws attention to that singular word, perhaps appropriate for the play. And it also suggests an interpretive shift towards war as the key setting, an allegorical or actual backdrop—rather than say, familial relations implied in the subtitle to the quarto edition of the play. The use of capitalization for emphasis in the Folio appears further down in the speech as well: the line "I, that am Rudely stampt, and want loves Majesty, / To Strut before a wonton ambling Nymph" (Folio) appears as "I, that am rudely stamped, and want love's majesty / To strut before a wanton ambling nymph" (1.1.16–17) in the Arden. In the Folio the prominence of "Rudely" appears in opposition to Majesty. Thus the printer of the Folio drew attention to the structuring of the speech around oppositions that can be deemed symbolic or thematic. The modern edition diminishes this role of capitalization. But such changes away from capitalization in the modern edition are not entirely modern. In fact, the first quarto (1597) of the play capitalized very few words in the opening speech, but the ones emphasized may be telling: beyond the first words of each line, the printer capitalizes Yorke (a proper name), Ocean, Ladies, Nymph and Prophecies. Notably, war is not capitalized; nor is majesty.

In recognizing these variations it is important to know that spelling and punctuation in Shakespeare's day were variable. Furthermore, we have no evidence that the spelling and punctuation in the printed versions of the play were approved by Shakespeare; it is more likely these choices were made by printers. It might be frustrating to learn that there is no definitive version of the play's typesetting, and that elements of the play's language that you'd like to draw attention to—capitalization, for example—are not as stable as they are in a modern text by a playwright like Samuel Beckett, who was notoriously fastidious about the printed editions of his plays. But by educating ourselves in these textual variations, we are better able to read the play with the kind of flexibility necessary to make our arguments as convincing as possible. And furthermore we are able, like Cordery, to say *why* we are paying attention to a particular version of the play. For an actor, using the capitalization as a guide makes sense. As literary critics, we might be wary of leaning too heavily on typographical features for our analysis.

One final comparison between Folio and quartos is worth our consideration. It has to do with punctuation. At the climactic moment of the play's final scene, Richard attempts to sleep in his tent before the Battle of Bosworth Field. He is plagued instead by nightmares, visitations from the people he has killed on his way to the throne. He awakes from this dream vision, panicking. Here are three printed versions of the speech from 5.3, the Arden modern edition, the first quarto, and the Folio (with the early modern letters, like v and s, from the quarto and Folio modernized):

> Give me another horse! Bind up my wounds!
> Have mercy, Jesu.—Soft, I did but dream.
> O coward conscience, how dost thou afflict me!
> The lights burn blue. It is now dead midnight.
> Cold fearful drops stand on my trembling flesh.
> What do I fear? Myself?
>
> (Arden, 5.3.177–82)

> Give me another horse, bind up my wounds,
> Have mercie Jesu: soft, I did but dreame.
> O Coward conscience, how dost thou afflict me?
> The lights burne blew, it is now dead midnight,
> Cold fearefull drops stand on my trembling flesh,
> What do I feare? myselfe?
>
> (quarto 1)

> Give me another Horse, bind up my Wounds:
> Have mercy Jesu. Soft, I did but dreame.
> O coward Conscience! how dost thou afflict me?
> The Lights burne blew. It is not dead midnight.
> Cold fearefull drops stand on my trembling flesh.
> What? do I feare my Selfe?
>
> (Folio)

Comparing these versions, we immediately see in the Arden edition—beyond its modernized typescript and more conventional spelling—the use of exclamation points to suggest Richard's heightened emotional state. The contrast between his two opening exclamations ("Give me another horse! Bind up my wounds!") and the pause inserted after "Jesu.—" suggests how he calms himself, reassuring himself he's only dreaming. But this comfort is momentary as he swings back to his conscience, and another exclamation. The quarto and Folio versions instead use commas and a question mark (with the Folio's one exclamation after "Conscience!"). As careful readers we might feel that the Arden text accurately adds a sense of emotional drama to the scene. But we might also notice that, were our analysis of the scene to hinge on the use of exclamation points, we would be interpreting not Shakespeare but Shakespeare's modern editor.

This is to say, as you begin to read and analyze the text, keep in mind that some of the interpretive features of modern century texts—like Samuel Beckett or James Joyce's use of spelling, capitalization, and punctuation, which are key to interpreting their texts—are more variable in the case of the Shakespeare text. For that reason, you are on safer ground when your argument depends upon word choice and syntax. For example, in the speech above, what indicates Richard's emotional state, beyond the punctuation? Plenty, and we will provide an answer to this question below, in our discussion of rhythm and meter.

For now, we can conclude our discussion of the printed history of *Richard III* by noting that the type of comparison of texts we have been doing here—moving from the quarto of 1597 to the Folio of 1623 to the modern edition—is made possible for you through digital databases like *Early English Books Online*. In essence the kind of analysis that editors used to do in traveling to various archives around the world, you are able to do yourself, from your desk. The editions I have consulted here—a quarto from the Henry E. Huntington Library in San Marino, CA, USA; a Folio from the Folger Shakespeare Library in Washington, D.C., as well as other editions from the British Library in London—are available on *EEBO* without traveling at all. This opportunity means that you are able to conduct the kind of high-level comparison and research that was only available to specialists a decade ago—and you are in the first generation of writers able to do this.

But such editorial comparisons are not, in the end, what draw most readers to Shakespeare. What interests most of us is the content of the play, its words, its characters and its action. In which case, knowing about the range of versions of the play—from quarto to Folio to modern edition—can simply help you build your interpretations of the play on the firmest ground possible.

Reading *King Richard III*, 1.1.1–41

Now, having surveyed some of the opportunities and pitfalls of reading the text, we can turn directly to the play and grapple in more detail with one of its most important speeches: Richard's opening soliloquy. Richard is Shakespeare's only character to open a play in soliloquy, and he speaks almost a third of the play's lines, dominating the stage from start to finish. As we analyze these forty-one lines, our goal will be to develop our skill at paying close attention to a speech—in terms of its specific words, its poetry, its structure—in order to analyze not just what Richard is saying in the speech, but how and why he's saying it.

Keep in mind: to Shakespeare's audiences, the historical king Richard III would be familiar—and notorious. Coming to see the play for the first time and even before hearing Richard's opening speech, audience members would know Richard as a murderer and usurping traitor, a man who killed his nephews on the way to stealing the throne. This version of the king had been made famous in the historical chronicles on Richard's life, written in the decades before Shakespeare's play and examined in the introduction to this book. Coming at the king's reign through Tudor historiography, the audience expects a villain.

Audiences would also know Richard from his character in Shakespeare's *Henry VI* trilogy. Here, Richard brags about how easy it will be for him to steal the crown from his brother Edward, given his own skill in transforming and plotting: "I can add colours to the chameleon / Change shapes with Proteus for advantages / And set the murderous Machevil [Machiavel] to school" (*3 Henry IV*, 3.2.16). It is worth pausing on Richard's term "murderous Machevil." The "Machevil" or "Machiavel" was known as an ambitious, self-serving, villainous figure, named after Niccolò Machiavelli, an Italian writer whose sophisticated range is reduced to a theatrical stereotype. While Machiavelli wrote a great number of books, including political theory on the Italian Republic in the *Discoursi* and comic plays like *La Mandragora*, he became infamous in England for his small book *Il Principe*, or *The Prince* (1532). This "how to" guide for rulers about gaining and keeping power argues in favor of duplicity, ignorance, corruption, and ambition. Machiavelli's argument became condensed into one famous sentence: it is better to be feared than loved. This recipe for tyranny—which circulated throughout Europe and into England—provoked responses from horror to admiration, and became notorious enough that by the time of Shakespeare's composition of *Richard III*, the Machiavel was a known stage figure, a villainous ruler who seeks and holds power at any cost.

Richard would also be known as another villainous theatrical type, the Vice. Richard directly references this figure when he tells us, "Thus, like the formal Vice, Iniquity, / I moralize two meanings in one word" (3.1.82–3). As with the Machiavel, the Vice has a stage history. A stock character in late medieval morality plays, the dramatic Vice was one of the most amusing and compelling figures onstage. Morality plays were composed mainly as allegories and generally staged a conflict between good and evil, as forces battled for the soul of the play's hero, often called Mankind or Everyman. The play's chief Vice might be called something like Myscheff (Mischief), as in the play *Mankind*, or Sensuality in the play *Mary*

Magdalene. Later writers referred to the character simply as the Vice, a sinister but often comic tempter in the service of the Devil. He could be, for example, a boisterous mischief-maker, dressed as a fool, and riding upon the Devil's back. Typically, he engaged in puns and practical jokes, and provided a good deal of slapstick comedy. He was, therefore, a very popular figure up through the sixteenth century. With a tendency to introduce himself to the viewers and announce his villainy baldly, the Vice provided theatrical model for Shakespeare in creating his own villain.

Now, having considered what readers and audiences might already know when the title character comes forward to deliver the opening lines of the play, let's turn to this famous speech:

Now is the winter of our discontent
Made glorious summer by this son of York,
And all the clouds that loured upon our house
In the deep bosom of the ocean buried.
Now are our brows bound with victorious wreaths,
Our bruised arms hung up for monuments,
Our stern alarums changed to merry meetings,
Our dreadful marches to delightful measures.
Grim-visaged War hath smoothed his wrinkled front;
And now, instead of mounting barbed steeds
To fright the souls of fearful adversaries,
He capers nimbly in a lady's chamber
To the lascivious pleasing of a lute.
But I, that am not shaped for sportive tricks,
Nor made to court an amorous looking-glass;
I, that am rudely stamped, and want love's majesty
To strut before a wanton ambling nymph;
I, that am curtailed of this fair proportion,
Cheated of feature by dissembling Nature,
Deformed, unfinished, sent before my time
Into this breathing world, scarce half made up,
And that so lamely and unfashionable
That dogs bark at me as I halt by them—

Why, I, in this weak piping time of peace,
Have no delight to pass away the time,
Unless to see my shadow in the sun
And descant on mine own deformity.
And therefore, since I cannot prove a lover
To entertain these fair well-spoken days,
I am determined to prove a villain
And hate the idle pleasures of these days.
Plots have I laid, inductions dangerous,
By drunken prophecies, libels and dreams,
To set my brother Clarence and the King
In deadly hate, the one against the other;
And if King Edward be as true and just
As I am subtle, false and treacherous,
This day should Clarence closely be mewed up,
About a prophecy, which says that 'G'
Of Edward's heirs the murderer shall be.
Dive, thoughts, down to my soul; here Clarence comes.

(1.1.1–41)

What we might notice, immediately, is the length of this speech. It is huge, forty-one lines long, longer than Hamlet's "to be or not to be" at thirty-four lines. Richard takes over the stage, before we've had a chance to meet any other characters in this historical drama. In offering such a substantial opening soliloquy, Shakespeare follows the model of Marlowe's *Doctor Faustus* and *Tamburlaine*.

Such an opening, we might notice, is more typical of Shakespeare's early-career style, which offers longer, declamatory, rhetorically poised speeches. By contrast, later in his career, Shakespeare shows a sophisticated ability to open conversationally, and perhaps more naturalistically. We don't tend, in everyday life, to offer such long speeches to ourselves; and Shakespeare, later in his career, increasingly opens plays as if we are eavesdropping on real-life figures. Think of some familiar openings: "Who goes there?," "When shall we three meet again?," or "Tush, never tell me." We begin with questions, or *in medias res*, overhearing a conversation. And most especially, we begin with secondary characters, not the titular figures.

Lest we begin to think, however, that the opening of *Richard III* reveals a kind of clunky, untheatrical, early-career awkwardness in Shakespeare, we might note, first of all, that Richard III is one of the most desirable roles for an actor in the whole of the Shakespeare canon. Part of this allure of the role comes, precisely, from this incredible opening soliloquy. What does Richard—and Shakespeare—accomplish here? This is not a soliloquy like some of Hamlet's, in which we hear what are coded as private thoughts. Instead, Richard seems to have an awareness of us, and seems to ask for our help in accomplishing his goals. As Adrian Noble, who directed the play for the 1988 RSC production tells the actor playing Richard, "you *need* the audience; Richard needs them" (Lesser, 1994, 149). Anton Lesser, who played Richard in Noble's production, puts it this way: "Many of the soliloquies are vigorously direct address, with Richard using the audience sometimes almost as he uses other characters in the play, to surprise, to shock, to puzzle" (Lesser, 1994, 150).

How to begin tackling this behemoth? We can begin with the first word: now. Henry Goodman, who played Richard III at the Royal Shakespeare Theatre in Stratford during the 2003 season, writes, "it is not for nothing that the word *now* recurs so often in this opening speech. It is not just the 'now' of the play's period setting; more importantly, for me, it invites Richard's knowing connexion [*sic*] to this audience, on this night, in this theatre—*now*!" (Goodman, 2004, 208). Kevin Spacey calls his documentary on performing *Richard III* around the globe, *Now: In the Wings of the World Stage* (2014). The story of Richard III is one preoccupied with the past—healing wounds and mourning deaths from years of civil war—and anticipating the future—the reign of the Tudor house, continuing up to the moment of the play's first productions during the reign of Elizabeth I. But Richard focuses us on the "now," the moment in front of us. He insists that history has not yet been made, that it is unfolding. For

Richard, history is in the making, as he undoes and redoes stories about himself and his family. Indeed, we might say that the play begins with the word "now" to signal Richard taking control of his infamous story, retelling it on his own terms.

The word, "now," resonates throughout the speech, and the play: "Now are our brows . . ." "And now . . ." leading up to the fatal announcement about "this day should Clarence closely be mewed up." The "now" facing the audience is treachery, and murder. If you do a keyword search on "now" using an online version of the play, you will begin to hear how Richard invokes this word to motivate himself and his allies. You will also hear it at the play's end, on Bosworth Field as Richard lies awake, haunted: "It is now dead midnight" (5.3.181). Henry Goodman argues of this "now" on Bosworth Field that "*now* it surely must be, taking us back to the play's first word, not the 'not' that one of the quartos presents" (Goodman, 2004, 216). Goodman here argues, based on the play's internal logic, that the word "now" makes more sense than an alternate word, "not," which appears in some editions of the play. And we might well agree: in the shift from the opening "now" to this closing act, we hear the transformation of Richard, from commanding the stage, the audience, and fate in the opening scene, to questioning himself and providence in the end.

If we turn to other keywords of the first lines, studied above in capitals, we can continue to tease out the meanings in this opening speech: winter, summer, son, clouds. These opening lines invoke oppositions: winter turns to summer; brows to wreaths; and arms to monuments. These oppositions are ordered and pleasing, delivering the good news of peace and success. What is stern and dreadful has become merry and delightful—with the word "merry" frequently signifying "drunk" in Elizabethan England. We are now, Richard seems to say, able to celebrate. These opening lines have a clarity of organization that lures us in, and puts us at ease. But are all of these oppositions equivalent or equal? To be more pointed, do you notice anything different about his invocation of "Grim-visaged war" when compared to the oppositions that come before? Read it above. The speech's initial oppositions hinge on mutually exclusive realms: alarums "change to" meetings. But this last opposition features a continuity: the figure of war, in smoothing his face, moves into the bedroom, from mounting barbed steeds to capering in a lady's chamber. This image is arguably more haunting than those before it, because it suggests not that war changes to peace, but that it merely changes location. And in doing so, we might argue, this image of war presages Richard's own behavior in the next scene of the play when he woos Lady Anne. A figure more comfortable with war than peace, Richard remains as aggressive and violent as he had been in wartime, but he shifts to a different register, smoothing his face to conquer courtiers ignorant of the danger they are in. So embedded in this allegorized image of war, we might say, is the trajectory of Richard himself: he too will move from the battlefield to the bedroom, but he will be a continuous force of destruction, whether his brow is furrowed or his face is smiling.

We might further notice Richard's distaste for this time of peace when he describes how war "capers nimbly in a lady's chamber / to the lascivious pleasing of a lute." Audiences instinctively laugh on hearing these lines, recognizing Richard's distain of such sensual, musical interludes. What cues us, that this line is dismissive and indeed funny? The alliteration of the letter "l," which we hear in "lascivious pleasing of a lute," resonates with the word "love," arguably evoked out of "la la la" of the sentence; and it also sounds, in its alliterative lisp (heightened in many performances) feminine. It is not what linguists deem a hard or masculine consonant, like "k" or "d" (and Richard loves to trade in such stereotypes). Richard makes a lisping sound in "lascivious pleasing" that he signals as a diminishment of masculine powers. Capering and lascivious and lute all indicate a kind of effeminacy to this peacetime that compromises war itself. Such mockery might make us uncomfortable, particularly if we don't concur with his stereotypes of masculinity and femininity; but Richard likes to ferret out his allies precisely by making some of his audience uncomfortable and others accomplices.

Looking back on the play's opening line from the vantage point of this long first sentence, we might now see or hear a kind of threat, not only to the court but also—potentially, and eventually—to us. Although Richard puts winter in the past—winter has turned glorious summer—nevertheless there's a way that he seems to be still dwelling in wartime, continuing a fight that should have been left behind. This threat becomes obvious as the regularity and balance of the speech's opening section shifts to a more oppositional stance, in which Richard separates himself from the "our" of the court and his family to an isolated "I." As Antony Sher reports, the Royal Shakespeare Company voice coach Cicely Berry teaches the speech "in three sections, the cue being in the opening two words of each section: 'Now is . . .' (the world like this); 'But I . . .' (am like this); 'And therefore . . .' (these things are going to happen)" (Sher, 2006, 193). David Troughton, who played Richard III in Steven Pimlott's production at the Royal Shakespeare Theatre in 1995 and at the Barbican in 1996, instead divides this opening speech into two styles of delivery: the opening style is a poetic statement of sorts, based in lyrical antithesis, while the second "more personal, colloquial, and direct" style emerges with the first line above: "But I, that am not shaped for sportive tricks." Troughton noticed, as an actor, the effect of these two styles of delivery: "one, the public, for the world in general, and the other, the more colloquial and confidential, when addressing the audience" (Troughton, 1998, 78). Whether viewed in three sections, as Berry suggests, or two halves, as Troughton sees it, the opening speech reaches a crescendo in one line: Richard's bold announcement that "I am determined to prove a villain." This line is a turning point to the plotting of the final section of the speech, and it is worth examining in more detail.

Determined to prove the villain

We have been examining some of the speech's keywords: now, winter, summer, war, lute. Now let's analyze one key sentence from the speech. When Richard directly addresses the audience with his villainous plans, "I am determined to prove a villain," he steps across the stage into the theater aisles. Directors have navigated this intimacy in different ways. One production put a velvet curtain across the set whenever Richard offered up a soliloquy, suggesting that the character stepped away from the stage set and into the theater itself to collude with the audience. In one film version we follow the character through the halls of the castle, into the bathroom where he delivers a portion of the speech as he pees. To consider the speech not in relation to staging but in terms of its language, we might concentrate on this one line itself. This line hinges on three keywords: determined, prove, and villain. The first, "determined," is a word that signals his intention—his determination—to become a villain. But it is also a word that, for Shakespeare's audience, would signal predetermination—a notion that Richard, from the start, is destined to evil. So the word works in two directions: it either signals Richard's immense will power, in shaping himself through grit and determination; or it indicates how Fortune or God has shaped Richard into someone destined for evil, someone who is reprobate rather than elect. In the post-Reformation world of Elizabethan England, the specter of reprobation—and the idea that someone might be damned from birth—was a haunting one. Even though the historical Richard III lived in Catholic England, before the rise of the Reformed Church and its election theology, the play nevertheless shapes his character through questions about predestination that are firmly sixteenth, not fourteenth, century. And one of the ways it signals this conflict—is Richard among the reprobate, damned from the start?—is through this word "determined," and ultimately, most powerfully, through the repeated phrase "despair and die" (5.3.140ff) at the play's end. Despair marked the one spiritual condition beyond hope for redemption.

The other keyword in this line is the verb "prove." Here, the word "prove" stands in complementary tension to "determined." If we look up the term in the *Oxford English*

Dictionary (OED)—an immense resource you'll hear more about as we go along—we learn that in Shakespeare's day the term signifies: "to demonstrate, to establish"; "to show the existence or reality of; to give demonstration or proof by action"; "to demonstrate oneself," or "show oneself by trial, action, or experience," or finally, "to become." To prove indicates a kind of unfolding, in which one reveals oneself to be something, through action. But as with "determined," the term "prove" leaves Richard's agency in question. Is he already a villain who seeks to demonstrate this fact to others, revealing his true nature? Or is he determined to turn himself into a villain, proving himself to be one where he had not been before? In one case, Richard has a firm identity, the villain; in another, he seeks to shape himself through action into the part he wants to play or prove.

Finally, the keyword in this line is, of course, villain. The stage villain, which Richard promises to be, has a long history. We rehearsed some of this above, in our discussion of the Vice and Machiavel. Shakespeare clearly had both theatrical traditions in mind when he created his villain. Richard is unapologetically wicked and is even accused of being an agent of the devil, as when Margaret calls him "hell's black intelligencer" (4.4.71). Yet Richard is an unusual villain. In the medieval morality tradition, the Vice figure was contained by the Christian frame of the play. Good angels, God, and Christ would eventually conquer the Vice. Yet Richard denies such a Christian framework. Further, in viewing himself as a Machiavel, Richard nods to a more modern tradition in which pragmatism and ambition trump religion. (Machiavelli was notably attacked as heretical.) If Machiavelli's theatrical double, the Machiavel, was like the Vice figure in several key respects—a character driven by worldly concerns and ambitions, appealing to the audience through humor—he was nevertheless more worrying in that he existed independently of a providential framework. In the Vice's medieval world, God's plan makes itself known in good time; in the Machiavel's modern world pragmatism, ambition, and cold scrapping win the day. In framing Richard's villainy through these two traditions the play poses the following questions to us: Is this a universe where a Machiavel runs rampant without a clear Christian ending or moral? Or does providence, in the form of Richmond and/or the ghosts, successfully vanquish the villain in the end? These questions will preoccupy us in Chapter Two.

Rhythm and meter

So far we have studied the printed versions of the Shakespeare text; and we have analyzed individual words, and key sentences. Now it is time to turn to the rhythm of Shakespeare, his music. Shakespeare writes in iambic pentameter, developing the "mighty line" that Marlowe relied upon in his great plays. Each line has five beats (pentameter) and it is arranged in two syllable units that place the stress on the second beat (iamb). We might hear this as a kind of percussive rhythm structuring the speeches. Actors certainly comment on this feature of Shakespeare's verse. David Troughton begins his process of learning lines by listening to them. In preparing his Richard III, he says "I then went through every line, 'Humpty-Dumpty' fashion. This is my word to describe the reading of any Shakespeare text obeying the iambic rhythm at all times—Di *Dum*, di *Dum*, di *Dum*, di *Dum*, di *Dum*" (Troughton, 1998, 78).

Troughton's point, that a play might obey "the iambic rhythm at all times," is appropriate for the opening speech that we've been analyzing in this chapter. This speech is a marvel of regularity. Each of Richard's opening lines is neatly balanced with an endstop (i.e. stops at the line's end), and some lines repeat an opening word ("our ..." "our ..." "our ..."), a rhetorical device known as anaphora that highlights a parallel, even structure. The speech features no enjambment (i.e. no stopping a sentence in the middle of the line of iambic pentameter). Not once does Richard interrupt himself, or stop mid-thought. We can hear the inevitable beating of the iambic pentameter in the first lines: "Now *is* the *win*ter *of* our

discontent / Made *glori*ous *sum*mer *by* this *son* of *York*." The
stresses draw out the oppositions, of winter and discontent to
glory and summer, highlighting the pun on "son" through the
stress on the word: it is the sun of summer, and the progeny of
the York house.

To hear just how regular this meter is, we might turn, by
way of contrast, to Richard's speech on Bosworth Field, his
"Give me another horse! Bind up my wounds!" (5.3.177). In
our above discussion of typesetting I asked, how might we feel
Richard's emotional intensity in this speech without relying on
punctuation as evidence, the exclamation points added to the
modern edition? Here is our answer: we notice the rhythm of
Richard's lines. He speaks, uncharacteristically, in short
sentences that stop in the middle of the line:

> Give me another horse! Bind up my wounds!
> Have mercy, Jesu.—Soft, I did but dream.
> O coward conscience, how dost thou afflict me!
> The lights burn blue. It is now dead midnight.

> (5.3.177–80)

Indeed, this speech in his tent on Bosworth Field stands out for
its choppiness, suggesting that emotion governs him, not
reason. He moves from a three-beat sentence to a two-beat
sentence in one line. Then he moves to two phrases that are two
and a half beats in the next line; the following line has an extra
beat, and thus is not traditional pentameter but hexameter. We
can hear, in these irregular lines, Richard's loss of control and
his heightened anxiety. This speech interrupts itself. Richard
darts back and forth in his imagination, questioning himself.
And we can use this point about rhythm to make our argument
about Richard's emotion without resorting to evidence based
on transitory punctuation. Noticing these variations in line
length and organization helps us to put our finger on what we
might instinctually feel, reading or hearing this speech: Richard
is at a breaking point. The former control he exerted over his
speech, his rhetorical mastery even alone with us, is eroding.

We feel this in the speech's shift from anaphora (the technique used in the opening speech, which feels like orderly repetition—"our," "our," "our") to a figure known as epistrophe, the repetition of a word or phrase at the end of successive clauses:

> Then fly! What, from myself? Great reason why?
> Lest I revenge. What, myself upon myself?
> Alack, I love myself. Wherefore? For any good
> That I myself have done unto myself?

> (5.3.185–8)

The repetition of "myself," far from seeming orderly and organized, instead feels anxious and hysterical—he is meditating on himself, and cannot answer his own questions. Is he a murderer? No, yes! Richard's speech ends with a newfound recognition, expressed through another kind of repetition, anadiplosis: it is the repetition of a word that ends one clause at the beginning of the next. He says, "My conscience hath a thousand several tongues, / And every tongue brings in a several tale, / And every tale condemns me for a villain" (5.3.193–5). Here, Richard's equilibrium may have been restored—he no longer speaks in enjambed, irregular lines, offering instead a metrically balanced and regular conclusion to his speech—but his conclusion is a deeply haunting one, the first sign of his own awakened conscience.

Returning to Richard's opening speech, we see it presents, in contrast to the play's ending, a different kind of challenge. His speech invites us in. We might say it lulls us into a kind of complacency, in its clarity and structure. He naturalizes the oppositions he invokes, moving from winter to summer, war to peace, as if such cycles were inevitable. But what about those moments when the rhythm falters? One of the first examples comes in the fourth line, which has an extra beat, forcing the actor to either swallow the final word "buried" or to draw it out and thereby draw attention to it: "In *the* deep *bo*som *of* the *o*cean *bu*ried." The iamb ends with the first syllable of the final word, leaving an awkward last syllable, left hanging, or requiring, for the sake of rhythm, a full extra iamb to the line: "buried" could thus be read with three syllabus (*burièd*). In either case, this final word is a stumbling block, and for obvious thematic reasons: the clouds louring on the house of York are not, we come to learn, buried at all. Just as the line doesn't end where it is supposed to, with five beats, so too does what's buried linger on.

We have another example of how rhythmic variants draw attention to crucial themes in the line about "fair proportion." The line contains an extra beat, and thus lacks the fair proportion of the pentameter line used earlier in the speech. Further, the line begins with "I, that," a unit that, depending upon pronunciation, receives either a double stress (a spondee) or, in an inversion of the iamb, a stressed beat followed by an unstressed one (a trochee). Either way, the line initiates a kind of stumbling: "*I, that am cur*tailed *of* this *fair* pro*portion.*" Here it is literally Richard, the "I" of the line, that distorts its fair proportion as a regular rhythmic line. So, too, with the word "lover," which provides an extra syllable in the line "And *there*fore, *since* I *can*not *prove* a *lover.*" That final syllable seems to speak to his incapacity as a lover, his inability to fit into the mold of the fair, well-spoken suitor.

One final observation about this opening speech: it ends with a rhyme, a technique that Shakespeare uses judiciously throughout this play to draw attention to moments of Richard's sinister playfulness. We can almost hear his glee as he tells us "about a prophecy, which says that 'G' / Of Edward's heirs the murderer shall be" (1.1.39–40). David Troughton, in preparing his version of Richard, was especially interested in these rhymes. He noticed the internal rhyme of one sentence, when Richard seems to desire reconciliation with his family: "'Tis *death* to *me* to *be* at *enmity*" (2.1.61); and he began to ponder the rhyme of "me" with the final "ty" of enmity. "Why was it there?" he asks: "Could it be the way Richard 'performs' to mask his real intentions, a device by which he amuses people and thereby throws them off the scent as to his true depth of purpose? A comic, after all, could not possibly be deemed a threat" (Troughton, 1998, 79). And, it turns out, the play is full of such rhymes, as when Richard successfully woos Anne and celebrates in his soliloquy: "Shine out, fair sun, till I have bought a glass, / That I may see my shadow as I pass" (1.2.265–6). Of this rhyming, Troughton writes, "These couplets seemed to endow Richard with a malevolence above and beyond his stated treacherous intentions. He appeared to enjoy not only the logistics of his evil intent but also the manner in which he expressed them" (Troughton, 1998, 79). Here I invite you to think of other villainous characters who seem to enjoy their cruelty through punning and mocking language—figures like Alex in Anthony Burgess's *A Clockwork Orange*, who chronicles the ultra-violence that he and his gang inflict on their dystopic world; or *Batman*'s Joker. It can be the playful wordsmith, mocking us with rhymes, that proves most sinister.

Fearing Richard

We have grappled with the words, the structure, and the rhythm of the opening speech. Now, in a move indebted to Emma Smith's volume on *Macbeth* in this series, I invite you to assess the following:

> Now all of my family's troubles have come to a glorious end, thanks to my brother, King Edward IV. All the clouds that threatened the York family have vanished and turned to sunshine. Now we wear the wreaths of victory on our heads. We've taken off our armor and weapons and hung them up as decorations. Instead of hearing trumpets call us to battle, we dance at parties. We get to wear easy smiles on our faces rather than the grim expressions of war. Instead of charging toward our enemies on armored horses, we dance for our ladies in their chambers, accompanied by sexy songs on the lute. But I'm not made to be a seducer, or to make faces at myself in the mirror. I was badly made and don't

have the looks to strut my stuff in front of pretty sluts. I've been cheated of a nice body and face, or even normal proportions. I am deformed, spit out from my mother's womb prematurely and so badly formed that dogs bark at me as I limp by them. I'm left with nothing to do in this weak, idle peacetime, unless I want to look at my lumpy shadow in the sun and sing about *that*.

This version of the opening speech is from SparkNotes, a student guide that "translates" Shakespeare for the modern reader. This rendition catches some of the thematic announcements we've traced above: the end of war turning to peace, and Richard's discomfort with this new time. But the speech also, in its effort of translation, inevitably loses some nuance. Take, for example, the shift from "son of York" in Shakespeare to "my brother, King Edward IV" in SparkNotes. For many of my students, the lineage of Richard is a stumbling block, and it can be helpful to be reminded of dynastic relationships and titles. But "son of York" is a phrase Shakespeare clearly chose for a reason. Why? Well, we might say, his audience knew the dynastic lineage and therefore would not need the help that we, as modern readers, require. In this sense, modern translations like SparkNotes can be helpful. Equally helpful in this regard is the introduction contained in most editions of the play, carefully laying out the dynastic relations. But there is a more obvious reason Shakespeare chose "son of York:" it is a pun, coupling the seasonal shift to summer sun with the dynastic shift to Edward's reign. "Son" and "sun" appropriately combine in the figure of a king. In a similarly flattening translation SparkNotes presents the image of "Grim-visaged War" as "we": "We get to wear easy smiles on our faces rather than the grim expressions of war." But the danger lurking in the image of War, as we explored above, is lost.

To point out another alteration: what difference does it make that Shakespeare wrote "wanton ambling nymphs" rather than "pretty sluts" of the SparkNotes version? Putting the sexual slur of the SparkNotes version to one side, what do we lose in this modern, colloquial translation, and what do we gain? At best, the modern translation allows us to hear the sexuality of the speech more immediately than Shakespeare: we do not tend to use the word "wanton" to describe lustful feelings, but Shakespeare did. The translation helps bring out this feature of the four-hundred-year-old language. But what do we lose? The word "ambling" is missing, a word that we continue to use in modern English to designate movement: we are ambulatory, and when we aren't we might need an ambulance to help us. In other words, to amble means to move, to transport. Why would Richard especially resent an ambling nymph? In his opening he catalogues all of his physical incapacities, precisely why he can't amble or walk as this young, desirable nymph can. She floats, he lumbers.

So this one word "ambling" signals Richard's resentment of such women, his hatred for their attractiveness and capacity. "Nymph" does similar work. He does not use the word "woman" and certainly not "slut," as SparkNotes suggests. He might have used those words—Chaucer loved such bawdy language, and Shakespeare does too, at times. But here he chooses a resonant word, one familiar throughout the plays: "What nymphs are these?" Theseus asks in *A Midsummer Night's Dream*; "Nymph, in thy orisons," Hamlet calls to Ophelia. A nymph, we discover in the *OED*, signified a class of semi-divine spirits, but also designated a beautiful young maiden, a damsel. What we might say, then, is that a nymph is an idealized woman, a partially-divine beauty well out of Richard's earthly reach. Furthermore, she is a woman in control of her own desire, with the words "wanton" and "ambling" signifying her own her ability to move toward her chosen mate, and presumably away from those who repel her. By contrast, the term "slut" registers a viewer's gaze, naming and potentially condemning a desirable woman; slut is a term used most frequently by others as a slur; it is less frequently used by a woman herself. Even if the term "nymph" might have stood as slang for a prostitute in Shakespeare's day (the

OED suggests this gloss on "nymph" was more common later in the seventeenth century) nevertheless the wordplay still requires that we recognize the semi-divine and independent nature of a nymph to understand his resentment. By contrast, the SparkNotes translation turns the female subject into its object—a pretty slut—and in the process misses Richard's fury at women who seem more capable and agentive than himself.

The player and the audience

Having carefully analyzed the key words, sentences, and images of the opening speech, we can now use our close reading skills to understand Richard's conversational speech, namely his dialogues with other characters. Throughout the play, he takes on and off a dizzying number of roles, displaying impressive linguistic felicity in the process. Indeed, Richard's use of acting is intimately tied to his capacity with language: he is able to play so many roles—loyal brother, wooing suitor, kindly uncle, and dutiful sovereign—because he uses so many voices. In this section we will work through some of the voices deployed by Richard, keeping our ears open for shifts of tone, as well as variations in meter, rhyme, and syntax.

One dramatic shift in Richard's mode of speaking comes just after his soliloquy. In his exchange with Clarence immediately after his opening speech, Richard moves from the careful rhetorical constructions of the soliloquy to a more informal, intimate address with his brother, expressed through questioning concern: "Brother, good day. What means this armed guard / That waits upon your grace?" (1.1.42–3), "Upon what cause?" (46), "But what's the matter, Clarence, may I know?" (51). As the audience, we hear this change of register, from the mocking rhyming couplet about snaring Clarence ("'G' . . . the murderer shall be") to such apparently sincere (but we know to be feigned) concern. Clarence, of course, does not hear this shift. Instead, he encounters Richard's sympathetic indignation at the arrest in the form of the above questions.

Further, he hears, as we do, Richard's speculations about the cause of the arrest: women. "Why, this it is, when men are ruled by women . . . We are not safe, Clarence; we are not safe" (1.1.62, 70). The Queen and her allies, "the jealous o'erworn widow and herself," are "mighty gossips" (81, 83) Richard claims. Richard uses a timeworn technique of forming alliances with one group through attacking another (a form of Henry IV's advice to his son, "busy giddy minds with foreign wars"). In this case, through a mixture of misogyny and aristocratic privilege, Richard asserts his intimacy with Clarence: we both, he seems to reason, distrust women's access to power.

A further radical shift in Richard's language immediately follows this brief exchange, in the famous wooing scene with Lady Anne, the former wife of King Henry VI's son Edward. This scene is entirely Shakespeare's invention. It features the macabre spectacle of Richard wooing Anne over the coffin of her father-in-law Henry VI. She begins the scene cursing Henry's murderer (namely Richard)—and she ends the scene agreeing to marry him. If perhaps improbable in real life, this scene is, in performance, simultaneously terrifying and funny. We cannot believe what Richard accomplishes; and he does it through his masterful rhetoric, a skill on display in his opening soliloquy, but even more exaggerated in its application here.

We have already introduced a few rhetorical terms to you: anaphora, epistrophe, and anadiplosis. Now I will offer a few more, to help you to hear Richard's ingenuity in his exchange with Anne. Rhetoric in its original sense means the art or study of using language effectively and persuasively. In his conversation with Anne, he demonstrates precisely this skill: using language to persuade. Deploying rhetorical devices to such a degree that his speech draws attention to itself, proving at once showy and potentially distracting, Richard uses linguistic expression to amplify his emotional range and increase his effectiveness. For example, Richard's use of stichomythia (single alternating lines given to alternating characters) indicates a kind of sparring to their exchange that he uses to establish their intimacy. Anne cries, "O wonderful, when devils tell the truth!," and Richard responds, "More wonderful, when angels are so angry" (1.2.73–4). Richard challenges Anne's dismissal of him, "It is a quarrel most unnatural . . ." and Anne defends her position: "It is a quarrel just and reasonable" (1.2.137–9). She barbs him and he barbs back; he barbs her and she retaliates. But at the same time, we also might notice the way in which Anne's lines come to echo Richard's. She challenges him, yet echoes him in the process, thereby diminishing her own voice.

This point becomes clearer when we notice that the scene begins with her long speeches—she offers 40 lines and then another 35 lines. But by the end of the scene she is instead mimicking Richard—this mimicry betrays her loss of voice, and anticipates what might otherwise be surprising at the end of the scene: her capitulation. The turning point in the scene occurs when he gives her the knife and asks that she murder him; when she balks, Richard envelops her in his oppositional thinking—if she's not willing to murder him then she must be willing to marry him. When she asks "I would I knew thy heart," and he replies "'Tis figured in my tongue" (1.2.195–6), we know that all is lost for her. For we know what she does not: Richard's language bears little relation to his interior life. His heart, in other words, is most certainly not figured in his tongue.

I should mention, as a compelling side note, that the wooing scene with Anne is one of Shakespeare's most discussed scenes. The range required of the actor playing Richard is enormous. Hugh Richmond writes,

> Anne's ultimate reversal of attitude from the opening of the scene may seem challenging in performance . . . but looked at closely, it is clear that the boy actor has only one switch to make: from ritual hostility to uneasy reconciliation, the latter expressed in the briefest of replies to Richard's imperatives. By contrast, Richard has run the whole gamut of vocal tones, from violence to egregious flattery, from black humour to funereal lament, from the coarsest cynicism

to seemingly sincere repentance. No scene better illustrates the fluency and versatility of Burbage . . . The scene, like the whole play, seeks extraordinary means to display the virtuosity of its star.

(Richmond, 1989, 40)

Here Richmond refers to Richard Burbage, the actor in Shakespeare's company who played the role. Indeed, as mentioned in the introduction, some theater historians posit that Shakespeare wrote the role of Richard III with Burbage in mind, because this challenging part requires an exceptionally talented actor with a versatile range. You might try reading the exchange aloud with a friend: can you capture its "gamut of vocal tones" as you read out the lines, moving from violence to flattery, humor to lament?

As in the scene with Clarence, the scene with Anne ends with Richard coming forward to address the audience, commenting on the action. These soliloquies only heighten the sense of Richard's verbal and theatrical skill. He moves from feigning to be a loving brother or adoring suitor, to taking off his mask: "Simple, plain Clarence, I do love thee so / That I will shortly send thy soul to heaven" (1.1.118–19), he tells us after Clarence's departure for the tower; and famously with Anne's departure, he offers his mocking, jubilant soliloquy: "Was ever woman in this humour wooed? / Was ever woman in this humour won?" (1.2.230–1). These first two sentences exhibit further rhetorical mastery: as we learned above, alliteration is the repetition of the same initial consonant sound throughout a line of verse, and its relative assonance offers the repetition or similarity of the same internal vowel sound in words of close proximity. In addition to the alliterative play with "w" and the assonance of "o" in woman, humour, and wooed/won, these sentences betray, as with the opening speech, parallel construction, deemed anaphora: the repetition of a word or phrase at the beginning of successive clauses.

The point in drawing attention to this range of rhetorical devices is not to read Shakespeare's text looking for precise examples of rhetorical forms, as enjoyable as that might be (it's a bit like a treasure hunt). The point is to be able to train your ear in a new way, to hear things that it might otherwise not. If we are able to hear that Richard is deploying these devices, we are more aware of the speeches in the play as constructed—as speeches that might *seem* natural in delivery, but which are actually quite skillful in their design. We may not know the name of every rhetorical figure, but we do feel its effects. We register how these figures communicate emotional shifts, and how they work to persuade not only the characters onstage, but also those of us sitting in the audience, or at our desks. And once we recognize the ways in which the speeches are carefully constructed we are in a better position to ask, *why*? Why, for example, does Richard begin his soliloquy with such well-constructed, rhetorically masterful lines? After all, a soliloquy is where one speaks alone to oneself, unfettered by convention. The mere fact of speaking alone should guarantee honest self-expression. Hence Claudius confesses to the murder of old Hamlet in a soliloquy; and Iago repeatedly announces his devilish plans in this medium.

With his two questions, though, Richard seems to address not merely himself, but the audience, as if to say, "have you ever seen anything like this?" "Can you believe it?" Facing us, speaking to us, he then confesses his plans in jaunty, colloquial language:

> I'll have her, but I will not keep her long.
> What? I that killed her husband and his father,
> To take her in her heart's extremest hate,
> With curses in her mouth, tears in her eyes,
> The bleeding witness of my hatred by,
> Having God, her conscience, and these bars against me,
> And I, no friends to back my suit withal
> But the plain devil and dissembling looks?
> And yet to win her? All the world to nothing!
> Ha!

(1.2.232–41)

Richard grants us a special position. We even, we imagine, hear him think. Take, for example, the word "ha." Here a line of iambic pentameter ends, in the first beat. The rest of the line remains empty. This creates a textual as well as a performative pause—this is a pause we even see directly on the page. The "ha" expresses genuine surprise, and he might pause because he is taken back by his accomplishment. And this pause also seems—as it certainly does for Iago, who also delivers a potent "ha!"—to encode the act of thinking. In the pause Richard would take time to ponder.

But the danger, once we begin to notice Richard's skill with language, is believing that we have unmediated access to his inner life—something that Anne mistakenly imagines in the prior exchange, "'Tis figured in my tongue." Richard might speak directly to us, but he's using the same rhetorical sophistication he put on display with Anne, the same linguistic felicity and range. He might be pausing not to think, but to pull us in. That's the effect of the pause in any case. Thus Richard's rhetorical skill, and his reasoned arguments, seem crafted to persuade not only others, but also himself and us. Furthermore, we might note, he does not offer us unfettered, free speech but instead a series of game plans, thought out or constructed with an eye to persuasion. We might know more than the characters duped by Richard, such as Clarence and Anne who are snared by this Vice in the first act. Yet we find ourselves, like them, drawn in by his brilliant *appearance* of intimate vulnerability.

After all, Richard needs us: this is a play in which we, the audience, play a part. Goodman puts it this way: "Richard is the only Shakespearean villain who starts his own play and then guides the audience through it—'it's about *me*, in *their* world, with *your* help'—and he becomes their hero and villain in one" (Goodman, 2004, 206). Indeed, David Troughton imagined that the audience was an ally of Richard's that slowly emerges as his externalized conscience. He writes that he "needed the audience itself to become an actual character; a character which had the power to influence and affect the direction that Richard

takes during his murderous assault on the English crown"
(Troughton, 1998, 89). As Anton Lesser—who played Richard
III in the 1988 RSC production—puts it, "so often the audience
is denied the role of eavesdropper, of secret observer, and forced
into involvement, into a mood of uncomfortable collusion"
(Lesser, 1994, 150). Sher's own experience bears this out. He
says, toward the end of preparations for the play, "What's
happening is that I'm surrendering to Shakespeare's Richard.
He *is* funny" (Sher, 2006, 196). I might end this chapter asking,
do we surrender to Richard, too?

Writing matters

Soliloquies

*Analyze one of Richard's soliloquies, considering the effects of
his self-characterization on the audience (i.e. how does Richard
describe himself, and how does he present himself to us?).*

Before writing, imagine Richard's goal in addressing us; think
about the purpose of the speech. You do not have to address
this issue of audience and purpose directly in your paper, but it
can be helpful to consider *why* he is speaking, before you start
to analyze *how* he is speaking. Then you might ask the
following question as you write: how does Richard structure
his speech? Think about his use of oppositions (war/peace,
heroism/villainy, male/female, human/animal) in the opening
speech. In your chosen speech, how is it structured? What is his
tone in addressing the audience, or rather, what are the different
ways we might read his tone? Does Richard attempt to enlist
us as sympathetic witnesses to his villainy, or collaborators?
Or you might consider issues of genre, namely what category
of play *Richard III* occupies. How does his speech relate to the
play's genre as a tragedy (whether you view it as medieval *de
casibus* or Aristotelian tragedy) or history (either providential
history exposing God's designs, or secular history charting

individual ambition)? Does it include elements of comedy, troubling generic classification? The challenge here will be to construct an argument about how the speech is constructed, or what it means—rather than just summarizing the speech itself.

Scenes

Pick a scene with significant variations in how Richard speaks and analyze the differences, using the techniques we practiced above: examine variations in meter, use of rhyme, and vocabulary/word choice (as he moves from informal to rhetorically informed speech, for example).

Here you might consider 1.1.70–162, as Richard addresses Clarence, Brackenbury, Hastings, and then us; or 1.3, as he addresses the court, speaks to himself, and then commissions the murderer of Clarence. Finally, 3.4, the Council Table scene, offers an especially rich study in Richard's different voices, as he engages with Hastings, Buckingham, and the Bishop of Ely. Again, the challenge will be constructing an argument out of these differences in Richard's speech, rather than offering a series of smart observations. In helping to shape an argument, you might consider the following questions: when does Richard's speech appear the most authentic? When he speaks most informally? When he speaks in asides and soliloquies? When he speaks to his allies or those beneath him in rank? Do we ever see Richard entirely unaware of an audience? One might argue that even in soliloquies and asides he's playing to an audience, even if it is just to us or himself. He is never simply "himself" or "at ease." Does he use certain types of language to himself or with us alone?

Dialogue

Analyze Richard's exchange with Anne in 1.2 in relation to his opening soliloquy. How does his success with Anne prove surprising in light of his opening speech? How is this scene constructed, and what does it reveal about Richard?

What do we learn in Richard's exchange with Anne that challenges his own self-characterization in the first scene? How is the outcome of this scene surprising? How is his language in his soliloquy, and here in his conversation with Anne, similar and different? This assignment is intended to help you understand the crucial relationship between speaker and listener in the play: the success of Richard depends on his ability to persuade onstage audience members, such as Anne, as well as his ability to woo (or at least implicate) us as the offstage audience. Here, you will want to construct an argument about the function or structure of this scene.

Genre

Aristotle in the *Poetics* offers the following comments on the tragic hero:

> A perfect tragedy should ... imitate actions which excite pity and fear, this being the distinctive mark of tragic imitation. It follows plainly, in the first place, that the change of fortune presented must not be the spectacle of a virtuous man brought from prosperity to adversity: for this moves neither pity nor fear; it merely shocks us. Nor, again, that of a bad man passing from adversity to prosperity: for nothing can be more alien to the spirit of Tragedy; it possesses no single tragic quality; it neither satisfies the moral sense nor calls forth pity or fear. Nor, again, should the downfall of the utter villain be exhibited. A plot of this kind would, doubtless, satisfy the moral sense, but it would inspire neither pity nor fear; for pity is aroused by unmerited misfortune, fear by the misfortune of a man like ourselves. Such an event, therefore, will be neither pitiful nor terrible. There remains, then, the character between these two

extremes—that of a man who is not eminently good and just, yet whose misfortune is brought about not by vice or depravity, but by some error or frailty. He must be one who is highly renowned and prosperous—a personage like Oedipus, Thyestes, or other illustrious men of such families.

Of the "bad man passing from adversity to prosperity" Aristotle claims "nothing can be more alien to the spirit of Tragedy." But this is, arguably, what *Richard III* offers. The play also offers "the downfall of the utter villain," a problematic and untragic plot that, even if it satisfies the audience morally, "would inspire neither pity nor fear." Consider the question of *Richard III* as tragedy, as its title page announces. Does the play unexpectedly inspire pity or fear in the manner of Aristotelian tragedy, even if it does depict the downfall of a villain? Might Richard be more complex than a mere "utter villain"? In other words, does the tragedy of *Richard III* push back against the Aristotelian definition of the genre, which insists that a play centered on a bad man cannot be tragedy? If so, how might you shape another definition of the genre, to account for Shakespeare's play?

CHAPTER TWO

Language and Structure

Chapter One focused closely on individual words, lines and speeches. Chapter Two concentrates on how the play uses language to construct its plot. At times we hear different types of languages spoken by characters, as we will find in comparing the prophetic utterances of Margaret to the pragmatic, bustling language of Richard, for example. At other points this difference occurs between Shakespeare and his sources, as he adopts historical chronicles on Richard III to create a complex and dramatic character.

Structure

King Richard III is organized into five acts, following the structure of classical Roman drama, and early modern theatrical convention. The tapers lighting the theater were changed between acts, marking the divisions between each segment of the play; so the five-act structure served a practical purpose, beyond signaling debt to a classical tradition. But thematically, this five act structure can feel a bit arbitrary, and in the case of *Richard III* there are other ways of organizing the play. Most obviously, the play might be divided in two, as Richard strives for the crown in the first long half; and struggles to retain it in the shorter second half. Let's examine this singular plot, of rise and fall, now.

Richard III, as mentioned, is one of Shakespeare's longest plays. Despite its length, however, the play's plot is straightforward in structure. Unlike many later tragedies with their complex subplots—the dual families of *Hamlet* or *King Lear*, for example—*Richard III* is monomaniacal in its focus on its ambitious hero. Its structure, typical of the medieval *de casibus* tradition explored in Chapter One, follows the hero's rise through four acts, and his precipitous fall in the fifth. Some scenes proceed without Richard and those scenes put pressure on the audience to notice the effects of Richard's villainy. But mostly, we are firmly linked to him throughout, and are given little opportunity to develop affection or sympathy for other characters until the play's end.

It is part of the strain of playing the role, this omnipresence of Richard onstage. Director Terry Hands described it like this:

> He [Shakespeare] doesn't give Richard a rest. Macbeth has the England scene, Hamlet has all that Ophelia stuff, Lear's got the whole Edmund sub-plot, but Richard is on throughout. With the terrible physical strain, of course, of sustaining a crippled position all evening ... It's a little known historical fact, but apparently after the original production Burbage said to Shakespeare, "If you ever do that to me again, mate, I'll kill you."
>
> (Sher, 2006, 42)

Think about the structure of the first act: we are alone with Richard at the play's opening, and then are introduced to Clarence briefly at the end of 1.1 as he is led away to the tower. By the end of the act he is dead. We then meet Anne in 1.2, a compelling character. But she disappears for most of the play, reappearing only in 4.1 before her death. Hastings, Catesby and Buckingham endure as Richard's allies for a good portion of the play, but they offer refractions of Richard's power rather than strong alterative points of view. Queens Margaret and Elizabeth offer the strongest opposition to Richard, and a later section of this chapter explores their effects on the plot and structure of the play. But they are unquestionably secondary characters to Richard.

Because the full printed text runs well over three hours in the theater, cuts must be made. There is, Scott Colley argues, something about the play that forces one to alter it (Colley, 1992, 3); it is, Julie Hankey writes, "long, confusing, elephantine in its ironies and relentlessly iambic. The eighteenth and most of the nineteenth centuries had no doubts that as it stood it was unplayable" (Hankey, 1981, 9). Stage history suggests that these cuts further amplify Richard's stranglehold on the plot. Indeed, the eighteenth-century actor, playwright, and poet laureate Colley Cibber produced an influential—and deeply trimmed—version of the play. Seeking a more compact structure and clearer focus conforming to eighteenth-century standards of neo-classical order and regularity, Cibber's 1699 adaptation of *Richard III* omitted Queen Margaret, King Edward IV, and Clarence's murderers, as well as abbreviating the scenes with Anne. If Cibber's version was not particularly popular with audiences during the first part of the eighteenth century, Garrick's rendition of the Cibber Shakespeare—which he used to launch his career in 1741—established its dominance. The result was an even more Richard-focused play, and Cibber's version—dominant in the theater for 150 years—continues to inform modern productions: "This rhythm of successive refinement of a simpler, bolder concept is a recurring pattern in the history of the treatment of *Richard III*" (Richmond, 1989, 51).

If the play does not develop through counterpoint—such as a scene of Hamlet and his family followed by a scene of Ophelia and her family—what moves the events forward? Richard's own plotting. Again and again, he tells us what he will do and he proceeds to accomplish it. We saw repetition at the level of word and sentence in the last chapter: "Was ever ... Was ever?" Such repetition also exists at the level of the play's plot structure: the repetition of Richard's murderous designs and their fulfillment. Richard plots a murder, he accomplishes it through counterfeiting and feigning, and then characters lament this murder in terms that recall prophecies from the start of the play. Clarence has a dream, Stanley has a dream; Margaret laments the loss of her family, and Elizabeth laments the loss of hers. All the while, Richard tells us what will happen and we watch it unfold: he tells us he will dispatch Clarence, and it happens. He tells us he will woo and discard Anne, and he does. Repetition also exists in how scenes themselves are structured. Notice how often Richard delays his entrance into a scene: he enters late to the family scene, as Queen Elizabeth worries about her husband's health; he enters belatedly into the scene of reconciliation, as King Edward encourages courtiers to make peace; and he enters the Council Table scene late enough that Hastings has begun to represent his viewpoint.

You might think for yourself of other repetitive structures in the play, at the level of repeated lines, repeated actions, and repeated imagery. What is the function of such repetition? One answer: we become increasingly wary of Richard. We hear him make preposterous statements and plans that turn out to be true, and thus we learn through repetition to be cautious about what seems unlikely or impossible. Yet this is a logical response to the repetition. Actual audience response suggests almost the opposite: the number of deaths, and his improbable success, can seem increasingly funny. We are so aligned with Richard that it becomes hard to see outside of him. The murder of Clarence takes up a full scene, and happens onstage as he pitifully bargains with the murderers. But the deaths of Anne, Hastings, Rivers, Dorset, Grey and Buckingham all take place offstage. And Richard does not directly commit any of them. Furthermore, he invites us to dismiss and mock those characters who offer emotional, grief-filled responses to the action. In watching Richard perform versions of the same act again and again—commissioning the murder of Clarence, Anne, Hastings, Dorset, Rivers, and Grey—we become hardened and increasingly complicit. Part of the play's humor comes with the phenomenon of repetition itself: hearing something for the first time is a different experience than hearing it for the tenth, as the parent of any toddler asking "why" or screaming "no" will tell you. What we took seriously, initially, becomes nonsensical or parodic through repetition.

Thomas More's Richard

Our allegiance with Richard might seem counterintuitive, given his self-pronounced villainy. But Shakespeare crafts his play to increase our intimacy with this villain, a point that becomes clear when we compare the play to Shakespeare's sources. Holinshed's *Chronicles of England, Scotland, and Ireland* (1577) served as Shakespeare's primary source. Holinshed's account is itself adapted from *The Union of the two noble and illustre famelies of Lancastre and Yorke* (1550) by Edward Hall. Hall's version is based on the *History of King Richard the Thirde* (1513) by Sir Thomas More. And More drew on Polydore Vergil, the historian commissioned by Henry VII to write the story of Richard III and his defeat.

These historical accounts resonate with one another in many ways, and all of them chronicle the history of Richard III in terms that emphasize his villainy and support the Tudor rise to power. Nevertheless, these histories also diverge from one another. Thus we know that even as Shakespeare derives his plot of *Richard III* from Holinshed's *Chronicles*, the playwright bases his depiction of Richard as a brilliant villain upon More's popular and propagandistic *History*. More (the author of *Utopia*, and made famous most recently in Hilary Mantel's *Wolf Hall*), wrote his history as a firm contribution to Tudor historiography, helping to bolster Henry VII's claim against this tyrant by shaping an arch-villain, a Machiavel. He describes Richard in these terms:

> Richard, the third son, [was] little of stature, ill featured of limbs, crooked-backed, his left shoulder much higher than his right, hard-favored in appearance . . . He was malicious, wrathful, envious, and from before his birth, ever perverse.

It is for truth reported that the Duchess his mother had so much ado in her travail to birth him that she could not be delivered of him uncut, and he came into the world with the feet forward, as men be borne outward, and (as the story runs) also not untoothed. . . . He was close and secret, a deep dissembler, lowly of countenance, arrogant of heart, outwardly friendly where he inwardly hated, not omitting to kiss whom he thought to kill; pitiless and cruel, not for evil will always, but for ambition, and either for the surety or increase of his estate.

(More, 1515)

This is a powerful, energetic description of the villainous courtier, and it makes More's history a page-turner. But it is also one sided. The twentieth-century detective novelist Josephine Tey illuminates precisely this point in her mystery *The Daughter of Time* (1951): her detective Alan Grant complains that More's account has "an aroma of back-stair gossip and servants' spying" (Tey, 1997, 72), so that "one's sympathy tilted before one was aware of it." This is because, as Grant puts it, the entire history is hearsay: "More had never known Richard III at all. He had indeed grown up under a Tudor administration. That book was the Bible of the whole historical world on the subject of Richard III—it was from that account that Holinshed had taken his material, and from that that Shakespeare had written his" (Tey, 1997, 84). Grant's suspicion of More leads to his bedside investigations of Richard's rise and fall, and his insight that the maligned king was framed.

Tey's novel revived investigations into Richard III's life, and renewed membership in the Richard III Society, an organization devoted to clearing the king's name of wrongdoing and salvaging his reputation from the accounts of writers like More. And we might say, rightfully so. For regardless of how we view Richard, we certainly notice how More's description works to distance us from him. He is caricatured for us by a narrator— we get a long list of descriptors, with Richard catalogued as dissembling, arrogant, hateful, pitiless, cruel and ambitious. We never hear Richard's voice. This is precisely the point—the charismatic murderer is kept at bay, at a distance that protects us from his allure. Our connection to him is mediated by someone else with strong opinions, shaping our response to history by telling us precisely what to think and feel.

Like More, Shakespeare underscores Richard's villainy, and so he, too, comes under fire from Tey's Grant and the Richard III Society. But Shakespeare's play is far from a piece of propaganda. For the playwright does much more than present us with a murderous villain. He presents us with drama. As a result, the play begins with Shakespeare's Richard taking control of his own story, as explored in Chapter One. Furthermore, Shakespeare's character has more texture than either side of the polarized legend: his character is not merely a one-dimensional Vice figure bent on killing, nor is he a maligned hero. Shifting the story from third person narration, as in his sources, to first person address, Shakespeare gives Richard a voice. "The historical figure who ruled England," Bernard Spivack writes, "dissolves into the theatrical figure who ruled the English stage" (Spivack, 1958, 395). More's narration disappears, the historical framing of Holinshed falls away, and we meet this notorious figure alone, onstage, speaking directly to us in the present tense, now.

It is our intimacy with Richard III that makes his character so memorable and haunting. Indeed, Richard is a character of such depth, and so far beyond the one-sided propagandistic caricature, that the founder of psychoanalysis, Sigmund Freud, spent time analyzing him. Writing on the character type of the exception—that person who always feels different—Freud suggests that we all wish we were both beautiful and strong, with heroic attributes ranging from the "golden curls" of the Norse god Balder to the strength of Siegfried, a heroic warrior in Norse mythology:

> Richard is an enormous magnification of something we find in ourselves as well. We all think we have reason to reproach Nature and our destiny for congenital and infantile

disadvantages; we all demand reparation for early wounds to our narcissism, our self-love. Why did not Nature give us the golden curls of Balder or the strength of Siegfried or the lofty brow of genius or the noble profile of aristocracy? Why were we born in a middle-class home instead of in a royal palace?

(Freud, 1964, 314)

Freud, far from distancing Shakespeare's Richard as a one-dimensional villain, instead finds him in concert with all of humanity. The struggles facing Richard are familiar ones, activating recognition and perhaps even sympathy in an audience. How does Shakespeare turn a caricatured villain into someone with enough depth to interest Freud? How does this murderer become someone who is, as Freud puts it, like all of us?

Freud answers this question, in part. Richard, he argues, appeals to our intelligence, forcing us to work to discover precisely what he's plotting. Through masterful use of confession and withholding, Shakespeare forms a character who is seemingly transparent, and certainly intimate with us, but who also keeps us at bay, as we labor to understand what's unfolding in front of us. Freud writes,

> It is . . . a subtle economy of art in the poet that he does not permit his hero to give open and complete expression to all his secret motives. By this means he obliges us to supplement them; he engages our intellectual activity, diverts it from critical reflection and keeps us firmly identified with his hero. A bungler in his place would give conscious expression to all that he wishes to reveal to us, and would then find himself confronted by our cool, untrammelled intelligence, which would preclude any deepening of the illusion.

(Freud, 1964, 314)

In other words, Richard excites us, he thrills us because he keeps us just that little bit in the dark. As a result, we are so busy thinking through his plans that we fail to respond to him ethically or rationally. From his opening "Now," Richard grabs us, offering a charismatic, energized, alive character, deeply connected with us, the audience—this figure is addressing us, overpowering us and the other characters onstage. And through this powerful role Shakespeare offers, as we will now explore, one of the earliest dramatic thrillers.

Thrilling Shakespeare

Penny Downie, who played both Lady Anne in Bill Alexander's 1984 RSC production and Queen Margaret in Adrian Noble's 1988 RSC production, describes *Richard III* in these terms: "the play is a classy thriller, no more, no less. It's got to go like the clappers" (Sher, 2006, 218). William Dudley, the designer on Bill Alexander's production, echoes this notion: "What we've got is a comedy-thriller in the best sense of the words. Vintage Hitchcock, if you like" (Sher, 2006, 242). This use of the word "thriller" by both Downie and Dudley illuminates something about the play: it is filled with suspense, anxiety, and excitement; with rapid pacing, villainy, and danger. We have already explored the play as history and as tragedy. But it is worth taking seriously this more modern generic term for it, to help illuminate how Shakespeare constructs such a compelling and even shocking play.

Vladimir Nabokov defined the genre of the thriller with characteristic insight: "In an Anglo-Saxon thriller, the villain is generally punished, and the strong silent man generally wins the weak, babbling girl." But, he goes on to say, "we always hope that the wicked but romantic fellow will escape scot-free and the good but dull chap will be finally snubbed by the moody heroine" (Nabokov, 1981, 16). Thrillers, Nabokov indicates, are usually plots driven by attachment to—or affiliation with—the villain, which is precisely what Shakespeare gives us in his version of Richard: we align ourselves with the murdering king at the expense of the dull savior, who enters at the eleventh hour with little charisma.

Here are the basic components of the genre, according to one writing manual on constructing a good thriller:

1   *You need a good story.* If Shakespeare inherited his story from the start, in the compelling narrative told by historical writers including More, Holinshed and Hall, he recognized and built upon this story's popular potential.

2   *Write about the underdog.* Richard casts himself as precisely an underdog from the first speech, telling us he is deformed and "sent into this world half made up," unshaped for the "sportive tricks" that occupy the rest of the Yorkist clan.

3   *Multiple points of view can give you a great range in a thriller.* Drama, of course, relies on multiple points of view, as we hear first of Richard's plotting, and then of the responses of opposing courtiers who attempt and fail to protect themselves.

4   *Open with an action scene.* The play does not begin, as it were, with a car chase. It is not the action scene of modern Bond films. But the play does begin with Richard telling us of his plans to murder Clarence and marry Anne—and he proceeds to do exactly that, an impressive amount of action for a first act.

5   *Early on, make clear what your protagonist wants and what he fears.* In the traditional thriller, the protagonist opposes the villain. He or she might fear, as with Michael Connelly's detective Harry Bosch, dark enclosed spaces after the experience of war—and thus might face precisely that environment in chasing a killer. In Shakespeare's version, Richard is both protagonist and villain: it is his own desires and fears that both drive him and come to undermine him, in the play's climactic scene before the battle of Bosworth Field. Freud helps illuminate what Richard wants, and

yet also fears: to be exceptional. Richard is different, and he wants this to be a sign of his superior power as he sits on the throne; but he also fears this difference as a sign of his unending isolation.

6 *Make your characters miserable.* Richard behaves as if his pain and misery is something he can take on and off; but the night before Bosworth Field reveals the degree of his torment. And it is this scene of misery, caused by his awakened conscience, that arguably is the climax of the play—not the moment of his ascension to the crown.

7 *Your main characters have to change.* This is one of Shakespeare's most significant contributions to the story of Richard: he changes Richard's perspective at the end of the play, invoking conscience as he wakes from his haunting dreams. This shift, from being feared by others to fearing himself, is a significant and unexpected development of his character. It deepens his range precisely at the moment of his downfall, securing our lasting sympathy even as we have realized his rule is unconscionable.

8 *Pacing must be high.* This is what Downie expresses above: the play moves like the clappers. No Shakespearean killer strikes as many victims as Richard.

Thrillers, of course, come of a variety of forms: spy thriller, science fiction thriller, mystery thriller, or as we have in the case of *Richard III*, a political thriller. Because of the wide range of types of thrillers, what truly defines the genre is emotion, as thriller writer James Patterson's introduction to the genre illuminates:

> Thrillers provide such a rich literary feast. There are all kinds. The legal thriller, spy thriller, action-adventure thriller, medical thriller, police thriller, romantic thriller, historical thriller, political thriller, religious thriller, high-

tech thriller, military thriller. The list goes on and on, with new variations constantly being invented. In fact, this openness to expansion is one of the genre's most enduring characteristics. But what gives the variety of thrillers a common ground is the intensity of emotions they create, particularly those of apprehension and exhilaration, of excitement and breathlessness, all designed to generate that all-important thrill. By definition, if a thriller doesn't thrill, it's not doing its job.

(Patterson, 2006, xiii)

The emotion of a thriller—excitement, apprehension—comes in a large part from suspense. We are on the edge of our seats, dreading what might happen. Alfred Hitchcock helps to explain the thriller's reliance on suspense (in which we anticipate an event, and fear it) over surprise (in which we are taken aback by an event), and his insights help us understand Richard's thrilling impact on audiences. Speaking in an interview about his art, Hitchcock says: "an audience experiences suspense when they expect something bad to happen and have (or believe they have) a superior perspective on events in the drama's hierarchy of knowledge, yet they are powerless to intervene to prevent it from happening." Think about our position with Clarence, or Anne. We know what they do not, and this knowledge puts us on the edge of our seats. Thus, Hitchcock claims, "Suspense relates entirely to causing an audience to go through emotions and can only be arrived at by giving them knowledge. . . . The who-done-it is an intellectual exercise like a crossword puzzle . . . The suspense story is giving the audience full information before you start" (Hitchcock, 1972). It is this dissemination of information, combined with the passivity of being in an audience, that produces the thrill.

Hitchcock gives very specific instructions on how to achieve this thrilling result through informing an audience of what might happen, and forcing them to watch the event unfold:

You and I sit talking and there's a bomb in the room. We're having a very innocuous conversation about nothing. Boring. Doesn't mean a thing. Suddenly, boom! the bomb goes off and they're shocked—for fifteen seconds. Now you change it. Play the same scene, insert the bomb, show that the bomb is placed there, establish that it's going to go off at one o'clock—it's now a quarter of one, ten of one—show a clock on the wall, back to the same scene. Now our conversation becomes very vital, by its sheer nonsense. "Look under the table! You fool!" Now they're working for ten minutes, instead of being surprised for fifteen seconds.

(Bogdanovich, 1963)

Dudley evokes Hitchcock in association with the RSC's *Richard III* above, and it is easy to see why he does. Shakespeare gives us this superior perspective, described by Hitchcock, from the play's first speech: we enter the action in the know, not only because we know the historical outcome of events, but more immediately because Richard informs us of plots and desires hidden to all the other characters but himself. We can begin to see and feel this intimacy from the first lines of the play.

Hitchcock's description perfectly accounts for the emotion in the scene of Clarence's murder, for example. We know what Clarence does not, that these men come to kill him at Richard's behest. So, too, with his marriage to Anne. We watch the scene of wooing governed by a sense of suspense—fear and anticipation—as he lures her, and plots to discard her later. Think of the Council Table scene: we know that Richard and Buckingham have turned against Hastings; we know that they will attack. It is just the thrill of anticipating how. The audience experiences the peculiar emotion of wanting to warn characters, not only Clarence, and Anne, and Hastings, but also the Archbishop who relents in releasing the princes from sanctuary; or Queen Elizabeth, who appears to consent to Richard's marriage to her daughter.

At the same time we feel a degree of affinity for Richard, the Nabokovian interest in a charismatic character. This charm of a villain, in the case of Richard, again conforms to what masters of the suspense-thriller genre acknowledge: "Most people misunderstand what a villain is. He's a charming man who kills women. If he didn't have the charm they'd run a mile from him" (Hitchcock, 1972). If More keeps Richard at a distance from us, we have a very different relationship to Shakespeare's Richard. He is intimate with us, cozy. He comes forward, directly addresses us before we've met any other characters, and delivers a behemoth of an opening speech. This intimacy with Richard might make us distrust and condemn him—it probably should, because he tells us upfront that he's no good. But instead Shakespeare also provides motivation, apparent interiority, and even sympathy for this character. He creates a character with a gigantic grudge against humanity, taking it out on everyone around him, and thrilling us in the process.

Alternative arc: Prophecies and curses

Shakespeare structures *Richard III* in the style of the best thrillers, charting the singular rise and fall of the villain. Yet we might, to return to the issue of structure, organize the play in yet another manner, in order to take more account of the other characters onstage: we could divide the play into scenes dominated by Richard, and scenes dominated or inhabited by other characters. This section will explore such a vantage point on the play.

Other characters, as we will see, share a language that Richard mocks or ignores: a language of dreams, prophecies, and curses. From the dream of Clarence to the prophecies of Margaret to the ghosts on Bosworth Field at the end of the play, this play invokes a supernatural world, even as it mocks such supernatural imaginings through Richard. In critical terms, these dreams and prophecies represent a counter-discourse, running against Richard's claims that he is in control of the plot. It is to this counter-discourse, offered by characters other than Richard and his ally Buckingham, that we now turn. In doing so, I'll be clear about terms. By prophecies and prophetic language, I mean predications, or divinely inspired utterances. By curses I don't mean swear words; I mean solemn utterances intended to invoke a supernatural power to inflict harm or punishment on someone or something. I'm connecting all of these because these are forms of language that are predictive, future oriented, and irrational. They are all forms of speech that are associated with the supernatural—whether dreams, alleged to come from God or the devil, to warn us or tempt us; or prophecies and curses, calling upon a higher power to make them come true. So this language is not based in will power or reason (like Richard's speech); it is a form of speech dependent on higher powers, and it presents a challenge to Richard—and to directors. Scott Colley, in his history of productions of *Richard III*, writes,

> Three central issues dominate every production of *Richard III*: (1) How can the actor bring Richard to life? (2) How is he to make the part his own while being haunted by the ghosts of the great Richards of memory? And (3) how is the company to balance the cosmic and earth-bound dramas that compete for attention during the course of the play?
>
> (Colley, 1992, 13)

This last point, on the play's cosmic drama, will occupy us now.

Our first example of dreams and prophecies comes in Richard's opening speech, when we first hear of the prophecy about the letter G. Richard's rhymes in this speech are, as examined in Chapter One, mocking, as if King Edward is naïve for believing a cooked-up prophecy. And the link of prophecy with naïveté is reinforced in the next scene: the king's willingness to be led by wizards, and women, betrays—at least according to Clarence and Richard—his weak rule.

CLARENCE
   He [the king] hearkens after prophecies and dreams,
   And from the crossrow plucks the letter G;

    And says a wizard told him that by 'G'
    His issue disinherited should be.
. . .
RICHARD
    Why, this it is, when men are ruled by women:
    'Tis not the King that sends you to the Tower;
    My Lady Grey his wife, Clarence, 'tis she
    That tempers him to this extremity.

                                 (1.1.54–65)

While this prophecy was indeed historically circulating—it started in a book of poems from 1476—Shakespeare has Richard run with the rumor, using it to his own purposes: for despite his indignation in this exchange with Clarence, Richard has already told us that he depends on this prophecy to manipulate the king. We are thus in an awkward position. Should we mock the prophecy, both because Richard is capitalizing on it and because prophecies are generally fuzzy and unreliable? Or should we believe the prophecy to be true, because, well, it *does* turn out to be true—Edward's children are indeed disinherited by a villain with the letter G in his name: Richard, Duke of Gloucester?

This kind of doubleness—should we take curses and prophecies seriously, or should we mock them?—appears again and again in the play's invocations of dreams, curses and prophecies. The play both asks us to question the power of such curses and, possibly, to take them seriously. For example, in the next scene, Anne offers a set of curses that seem at once impotent and yet eventually accurate:

    O, cursed be the hand that made these holes;
    Cursed the heart that had the heart to do it;
    Cursed the blood that let this blood from hence.
    More direful hap betide that hated wretch
    That makes us wretched by the death of thee
    Than I can wish to wolves, to spiders, toads,
    Or any creeping venomed thing that lives.

If ever he have child, abortive be it,
Prodigious, and untimely brought to light,
Whose ugly and unnatural aspect
May fright the hopeful mother at the view,
And that be heir to his unhappiness.
If ever he have wife, let her be made
More miserable by the death of him
As I am made by my poor lord and thee.

(1.2.14–28)

Anne casts a kind of spell on Richard when she repeats "cursed" multiple times. She also, we realize later in the play, is cursing herself—she will end up being Richard's wife, she will end up dying an unnatural death. As Richard says, "I'll have her, but I will not keep her long" (1.2.232). This scene seems to ask us to dismiss her curses—they seem like lamentations, not predictions. She is a character isolated and out of favor (which may explain why she capitulates to Richard). But ultimately these curses do come to pass, in slightly twisted ways: Richard's wife is indeed "miserable," and Richard himself is, like the child she imagines he might produce, marred by "ugly and unnatural aspect."

Powerless figures outside of the court also draw on prophetic language. We have a brief glimpse into the lives of citizens in Act 2, scene 3, as they consider the troubling events at court, and how these changes might affect them. And they offer a fairly grim prediction of their futures, seeming to implicate themselves—and certainly all of England—in the "storm" of Edward's death and Richard's rule: "All may be well; but if God sort it so, / 'Tis more than we deserve" (2.3.36–7), the first citizen cries; the other citizen replies, "By a divine instinct, men's minds mistrust / Ensuing danger ... But leave it all to God" (42–5). Their turn toward God seems, in the context of the play, a mixture of naïveté, resignation, and insight. They feel responsible for the danger at court, despite their distance from political events. We know the agent of misery to be Richard, making their resignation and contrition a moving counterbalance to Richard's recklessness. Thus these citizens remind us of a kind of piety otherwise missing from the play: they posit an afterlife and higher power that Richard entirely ignores.

Despite the truth of the G prophecy and Anne's curses, and despite the insight of the citizens, nevertheless Richard invites us—quite effectively—to mock these gullible characters. Shakespeare shapes a charismatic hero who asks us to laugh with him at others—at the incarcerated, women, and poorer men. One of the ways that Shakespeare achieves this split—between our allegiance to Richard, and our suspicion that prophecies are in fact true—is through Richard's own language. Scott Colley puts it this way: "not only does Richard appear and speak more than anyone else, he also speaks unlike anyone else. When others are formal and rhetorical, he is colloquial; when others are wooden and ponderous, he is witty and quick" (Colley, 1992, 6). So, before exploring the most dramatic and extensive prophecy in the play, uttered by Queen Margaret, we will take a moment to understand just how Richard manages to mock the play's dreamers and divines so effectively.

Bustling

When Richard plots the demise of Clarence and King Edward in his opening speech, he uses a range of techniques that make us accept and even collude with the unthinkable: murder. Obviously, Richard is funny, as when he claims "Simple, plain Clarence, I do love thee so / That I will shortly send thy soul to heaven" (1.1.118–19). This line always gains laughs in the theater. It constructs an opposition—between the "simple, plain" brother who is vulnerable and disposable; and the plotting villain who will thrive. What side do we choose? That of the disposable simpleton or the crafty survivor? This oppositional logic appears in his language of stereotyping more broadly, as when he uses misogyny to craft an alliance with Clarence; they are two brothers allegedly endangered by ambitious women. Read through the play with an ear to this language of building alliances through stereotypes and prejudices. Such oppositional language is Richard's bread and butter, and he uses it to often humorous effect: we chuckle at Richard's insinuation against women, knowing that he adopts such misogyny as a smokescreen for his villainy.

Beyond humor Richard deploys earthy language. Specifically, his speech can be colloquial and jaunty, in sharp contrast to the speech of other characters, as in his, "Ha!" (1.2.238; 1.3.233), or his statement to Clarence's murderers, "I like you, lads. About your business straight" (1.3.353). Within the broader language of the play, this aspect of his speech is unusual—it's striking, it stands out. In his first speech, for example, Richard insists that the world is his "to bustle in," when he claims "God take King Edward to His mercy, / And leave the world for me to bustle in" (1.1.151–2). Bustle is an unexpected word. We can use the *Oxford English Dictionary* to look up the etymology and the history of this word. And in doing so, we learn that this is a purely English word. It is, unusually, not derived from Latin or German origins. The word is defined as "to be fussily or noisily active; to move about in an energetic or busy manner; to make a show of activity. Often with *about*, *along*, *up and down*, etc." Bustle is an energetic word; it is a word about movement combined with activity. And thus "bustle" is a surprising word for a man who has just insisted upon physical incapacity as his defining attribute. Bustle is also, in its secondary definitions, linked to fighting: "to struggle, scuffle; to contend (*with*, *for*)." Or "to bestir, stir, rouse (a person or thing)." This range of definitions gives us a strong sense of Richard's own range: he is at once mobile, moving across the stage, and energetically plotting; but he is also creating conflict, rousing up courtiers and contending for the crown. It is, as we have already learned, such range that distinguishes Richard from the play's other characters.

One more point about bustle: it is also, arguably, vague. What does it mean, that he wants to bustle? Notice, he has not told us what we might already know: he seeks the crown. Instead, he tells us only that he wants to be rid of his brother for his own secret reason. This word suggests how he uses his own energy and ingenuity to make his way in a political landscape. His language is jaunty, colloquial and prejudicial; it also depends on everyday metaphors, as when he plots Clarence's death, so "George be packed with post-horse up to heaven" (1.1.146), or when he pauses to remind himself, "I run before my horse to market" (160). He was, as he claims to Margaret of his service to King Henry VI, a mere "packhorse in his great affairs" (1.3.121). A post-horse—another word formed within English itself, through compounding words—was the Renaissance equivalent of a taxicab: it was a horse kept at an inn to transport travelers or riders with the post or mail. A pack-horse is a bearer of burdens, a moving truck of sorts. Such quotidian images of mail horses, or town markets, are drawn from the everyday lives of audience members, not from the grandeur of royal courts. Richard's images, in other words, reach across the stage and into the yard and stalls, creating a sense of kinship between everyday people and this aristocratic courtier. Furthermore we might consider how, in deploying a specifically English vocabulary, namely words that originate in English and reference everyday life, Richard appeals to a nationalist logic—a sense of Englishness—that he later draws on to defend himself against interlopers to the court or foreign powers in the form of Richmond coming from France.

Notably, Richard does not rely on metaphysical or religious imagery, which he mockingly invokes as the province of others: as he says, "God take Edward . . .". Instead, he tells us directly that he only feigns faith: "I clothe my naked villainy / With odd old ends, stol'n forth of Holy Writ, / And seem a saint when most I play the devil" (1.3.335–7). In other words, God and the bible only serve as props for his dissembling. For other characters, though, the world of the divine, the futuristic, and the metaphysical is paramount.

Margaret's prophecy

In quick succession after the prophecy with Clarence and the curses of Anne, the play gives us the granddaddy of all curses in the history of Shakespeare: Margaret's long diatribe against the court in Act 1, Scene 3. This is the scene in which the current queen, Elizabeth, is bickering with Richard, who has been appointed Lord Protector: Richard insinuates that the queen's family are all social climbers, using her marriage to get positions at court, while Elizabeth accuses Richard of hating her family and undermining them. Enter Queen Margaret, the lingerer from the other side, a banished Lancastrian who haunts the court like a ghost. And she comes to offer this chilling list of prophecies:

> Can curses pierce the clouds and enter heaven?
> Why then give way, dull clouds, to my quick curses.
> If not by war, by surfeit die your king,
> As ours by murder, to make him a king.
> —Edward thy son, that now is Prince of Wales,
> For Edward our son, that was Prince of Wales,
> Die in his youth, by like untimely violence.
> Thyself a queen, for me that was a queen,
> Outlive thy glory, like my wretched self.
> Long mayst thou live to wail thy children's death
> And see another, as I see thee now,
> Decked in thy rights, as thou art stalled in mine.
> Long die thy happy days before thy death,
> And, after many lengthened hours of grief,
> Die neither mother, wife, nor England's queen.
> —Rivers and Dorset, you were standers-by,
> And so wast thou, Lord Hastings, when my son
> Was stabbed with bloody daggers. God, I pray Him,
> That none of you may live his natural age,
> But by some unlooked accident cut off.

(1.3.194–213)

These are difficult lines to deliver. They are, as Penny Downie puts it, breathless: "Her cursing speeches in this first scene follow such a rhythm that I found I had to work hard on my breathing. You have to push through to the end, take four-line thoughts on one breath, or it won't make sense. The speeches felt like arias to me, and if you take on board their energy you are sustained by it" (Downie, 1994, 135). This operatic quality of Margaret's speech suggests its role as incantation: she overwhelms the audience with sound and rhythm of cursing.

Martine Van Elk's account of the play's prophetic language— in the mouth of Margaret, but also from Elizabeth, the Duchess of York, and Anne—helps illuminate the challenge facing both the audience, and the actors playing these roles:

> The repetitive formal poetry of the curses and prophecies, often aligned with women in the play, is on the side of divine providence as well, forging not only a model of subjectivity that is devoid of agency but also a language that has become utterly a matter of ritual form, rather than individual expression. The question students need to answer is whether they feel that this apparatus of curses, puns, prophecies, and repetitive poetry effectively undoes the threat to order posed by Richard's improvisations. And if this is the case, should we be happy with this victory? Our modern sensibilities tend to make us feel more comfortable with Richard's evil but entertaining machinations than with the sinister wailing and cursing of the women in the play. Can we even relegate their fierce language to the realm of providence and if so, is it a kind of providence that appeals to us?

> (Van Elk, 2007, 10)

Margaret speaks in a very different key from Richard, calling on the divine, and seeking to "enter heaven" with her speech. And this different key can, as Van Elk illuminates, be off-putting to modern audiences, who feel more comfortable with Richard's individual, and improvised, language. Margaret's formalistic rhetoric seems devoid of such individual expression; she does not bustle, but instead offers a voice from beyond.

Margaret's repetitious, highly rhetorical language is also, as Lynne Magnussen explores, explicitly feminized in the play: she speaks as the other women speak, in "godly optatives" (namely performative speech acts asking for divine intervention). Such godly optatives would have been familiar to Shakespeare from his English grammar school and thus associated with male (specifically young boy's) speech in an educational setting. She writes:

> For wishing or desiring, schoolboys were instructed in a particular grammatical mood—the optative mood—that required considerable effort to memorize, decline, construe, and recite out loud in all its various persons and tenses. Ironically, Shakespeare creates a distinctive language of female passion in the English of this play that is strongly reminiscent of and highly evocative of schoolboy Latin grammar training—that is, he creates women's emotive utterance out of the experiences that have been most forcefully identified as the masculine puberty rites of Elizabethan culture.
>
> (Magnussen, 2013, 32)

This prophetic language is thus evocative for Shakespeare's audience in a way it might not be for us now: it encodes educational achievement, extensions of sympathy, role playing and one's emergence as an adult. And it is out of this language that Shakespeare creates his female laments, which are not evident in the play's sources and are one of his most noticeable inventions. Anne, Queen Elizabeth, the Duchess of York, and most obviously Margaret all speak in this style. As a result, Shakespeare shaped "an alternative form of potency in his female characters' speech acts" (Magnussen, 2013, 32).

If Margaret is driven by emotion and formal rhetoric, while Richard seems more calculating and individual (even as he deploys formal rhetoric to persuade), we might nevertheless notice some similarities in their manner of speaking: Margaret, like Richard, speaks in repetition. She is doubling back, saying for my king, your king; for my Edward, your Edward. I suffered and now you will suffer, precisely Richard's logic on opening the play. Margaret's mode is also familiar from Shakespeare's canon more broadly, in his range of characters who are marginalized from power. One of the more immediate examples is Shylock in *The Merchant of Venice*, whose beloved speech "Hath not a Jew hands, eyes, organs?" culminates in the notion of revenge: I suffer and so will you. Shylock's speech moves us. But it is also marked in the play as an Old Testament call for revenge and retribution, against the New Testament plea for mercy by Portia (itself a problematic plea; see Lemon, 2011). Indeed, revenge in Shakespeare's canon has a shaky and insecure logic: Hamlet spends an entire play questioning the call to revenge, while *Titus* demonstrates revenge's horror. So as much as Margaret's curses might move us, they might also unnerve us. Even Margaret finds herself cloyed by her calls for revenge: as she says in her last lines, "I am hungry for revenge, / And now I cloy me with beholding it" (4.4.61–2). Downie notes, "I used to get a sort of buzz in rehearsal as I heard her prophecies come true—Rivers and Vaughan, Stanley, Buckingham—a sense of Margaret ticking them all off on her list. So why does she not stay to hear Richard's doom? Why is she 'cloyed' with revenge?" (Downie, 1994, 137). Ultimately, watching other characters in pain does not assuage her own grief.

As with Clarence, Richard cues us how to respond to this character. His brother was simple and plain; Margaret is, he tells us, a "foul wrinkled witch" (1.3.163), a "hateful withered hag" (214). And in performance, Margaret often appears as mad, insane with grief or fury, problematic in her desire for violence. As Downie claims, "the main reaction to my news of having taken the part was always 'O, mad Margaret. You're playing mad Margaret are you?'" But Downie finds such responses to Margaret simplistic, saying "I'd ... had some experience of playing a mad character, but it quickly became clear that to call Margaret simply mad is a crude reduction of her complexity" (Downie, 1994, 115). Part of what makes Margaret so complex, according to Downie and other actresses like Peggy Ashcroft who have played her, is "her foreignness, her originality, her not-quite-belonging (in England, and later, when she returns there, in France too). She's out of place, and also out of time" (Downie, 1994, 115).

Despite our complex emotional response to Margaret's curses—wary of calls for revenge, and cued to mock her from Richard—we come to realize, slowly along with all the other characters in the play, that she speaks the truth: she says that King Edward will die of ill health, as he does; she claims that prince Edward will die young, as he does (at the hands of Richard); she warns that the queen will live on, fallen from power, mourning her dead children, as she does. She predicts that the various courtiers, Rivers, Dorset, and Hastings, will all die unnaturally, and they do; and that Buckingham will be injured at the hand that feeds him, namely Richard. These characters spend the rest of the play recalling her curses: Rivers, Vaughan and Grey invoke Margaret's curses as they are led to death, with Grey lamenting, "Now Margaret's curse is fall'n upon our heads" (3.3.14); Hastings recalls Margaret's curses, crying "O Margaret, Margaret, now thy heavy curse / Is lighted on poor Hastings' wretched head!" (3.4.91–2); and finally Elizabeth references Margaret's curses, asking "make me die the thrall of Margaret's curse, / Nor mother, wife, nor England's counted queen" (4.1.45–6). These repetitions serve to remind us, the audience, of Margaret's prophetic power against Richard's rising political power: what had seemed the lunatic voice of a grief-stricken, exiled, powerless woman seems increasingly a divinely inspired or informed prediction.

Margaret and Richard

It is this bass note, this repeated articulation of Margaret's speech, that provides a second spine through the play, rivaling Richard's own willful rise to power. One might even argue that the play offers, in the form of Margaret, a second hero who shadows Richard: she is a character whose fall brings her rise, at least in terms of moral high ground, while Richard is the character whose rise begets his fall. The play thus unexpectedly offers a double plot: the Richard plot, of his rise to power; and a second plot that runs through it, the prophetic plot.

The crucial role of Margaret in Shakespeare's play comes into clearer focus when we learn that she was added against historical record. The historical Queen Margaret left England shortly after November 13, 1475, and died on August 25, 1482. But her scene of prophecies cannot be dated before April 9, 1483. So her inclusion in the play is a construction, done for dramatic effect. Shakespeare's sources do not include Margaret at this point in Richard's trajectory. Yet Edward Hall's *The Union of the two noble and illustre famelies of Lancastre and Yorke* (1550) does include an evocative description of this historical Margaret, which may have influenced Shakespeare. Below is part of Edward Hall's description of Margaret, taken—and updated, with modern spelling and punctuation—from Siemon (2009):

> She much lamented, and bewailed the evil fate and destiny of her husband, which eminently before her eyes, she saw to approach. She accused, reproved, and reviled, and in conclusion, her senses were so vexed, and she so afflicted, and caste into such an agony, that she preferred death before life . . . and peradventure for this cause, that her interior eye saw privily, and gave to her a secret monicion [intimation of danger] of the great calamities and adversities, which then did hang over her head, and were likely incontinent to fall and succeed (which other persons neither looked for nor regarded).

> (Siemon, 2009, 65)

Reading Hall's Margaret and then Shakespeare's helps us to see the dramatist at work, adapting and expanding his sources, and shaping his haunting character. Hall's figure imagines "great calamities and adversities" in the future, ones "which other persons neither looked for nor regarded." In Shakespeare's hands this descriptive view of the prescient former queen, a kind of Cassandra figure, turns into a dramatic scene dominated by her own voice. Hall tells us that she "accused, reproved, and reviled" others, but Shakespeare shows us precisely *how* she does it, and in what terms. The result is a line of overtly-stated prophecies that come true one at a time. Shakespeare uses Margaret as an emotional and structural counterbalance to Richard in the play, because she alone turns out to know the future, even if it is a future out of her control.

What we might call the play's two heroes, and their two plots, chiastically intersect—meaning, they cross each other, as one heads up and the other down—midway through the play: Richard begins to fall and Margaret's prophetic voice rises as characters repeatedly invoke her. Here is Margaret's prediction for Richard, which comes to haunt him:

Stay, dog, for thou shalt hear me.
If heaven have any grievous plague in store
Exceeding those that I can wish upon thee,
O, let them keep it till thy sins be ripe,
And then hurl down their indignation
On thee, the troubler of the poor world's peace.
The worm of conscience still begnaw thy soul;
Thy friends suspect for traitors while thou liv'st,
And take deep traitors for thy dearest friends;
No sleep close up that deadly eye of thine,
Unless it be while some tormenting dream
Affrights thee with a hell of ugly devils.

(1.3.215–26)

And, as with the earlier curses, these threats to Richard play out before us onstage. He suspects Buckingham as a traitor, which he is not; he takes Stanley and Queen Elizabeth for allies, which they are not; he cannot sleep before Bosworth Field, enduring instead a haunting nightmare of his murdered enemies cursing him. And, most unexpectedly, the "worm of conscience" does afflict his soul in the end. What had seemed impossible—and indeed incomprehensible, for a character such as Richard who mocks the divine—comes to fruition. Simon Russell Beale puts it this way: "He [Richard] doesn't have the isolated malice of an Iago; Richard has a bout of conscience right at the end, which Iago doesn't. He just played the game. And then when the crown is on his head, it's not as much fun as he thought it was going to be" ("Richard III: Shakespearean Actors . . .," 2013).

One way of understanding such a double plot—between the bustling of Richard and the cursing of Margaret—is temporally. The two plotlines within this play operate on two separate time schemes. The Richard plot operates on the time indicated by his first word in the play: now, the immediate future being his furthest vantage point. The language of prophecies deployed by the other characters seems futile and powerless in this short term. But viewed from a long time scheme, these prophecies are powerful and accurate, and this second time scheme, of historical determination and inevitability, wins the day. But slowly and at great cost.

This temporal difference—of *now* versus *later*—maps onto an historical narrative. The play seems poised, as critics often comment, between medieval and modern England. As Antony Sher reports, "The death of the real Richard III in 1485 marked the end of the medieval world and the beginning of the Tudors and Modern English History. Up until then there had been an unshakeable belief in the control of God; now was the beginning of Humanism, of doubt, curiosity" (Sher, 2006, 169). This split between the medieval and the modern works on another level in the play, however. For Shakespeare's Richard, even though he might emerge from the medieval Vice, is unquestionably a modern character of business, bustling, and ambition; his world evokes Machiavelli and godless modernity. Against his Machiavellian and/or modern sensibility lies the play's older medieval world—of prophetic speech, and supernatural invocations. Predominately female characters speak in oaths and curses, and the play frames these women as powerless and, to a certain extent, outdated. Time has marched past them. All they can do is sit and worry, while Richard acts and plots. Ultimately, however, it is those characters who listen to the supernatural who survive. Queen Elizabeth and her daughter, like Stanley and Richmond, are alive at the end of the play. What, then, are we to make of the play's depiction of the medieval vs. modern vantage point? If Richard represents a version of modernity, his version arguably fails, leaving the medieval voices of prophecy triumphant—or at least alive. The providential reading of history triumphs both because Margaret's curses come true, and because Richmond enters as a *deus ex machina*, resolving conflicts and restoring peace. Perhaps this is part of the play's argument for Richmond: his foreign invasion, and attack on a sitting king, is not innovative but traditional. He stands for England's medieval past, even as he ushers in its Tudor future, suggesting time is not linear but cyclical.

Case study: Clarence's dream

This chapter has examined the play's opposing plots and languages, moving between the colloquial, jaunty language of a modern Richard and the prophetic curses offered by the medieval, religious characters. Now let's turn to a scene that radically toggles between these forms of speech, creating a dizzying effect for the audience. In the scene of his death, Clarence recounts in lush imagery his dream about Richard. His speech is notable because, as Jeremy Lopez puts it, "the amount of time and words given to Clarence and his anonymous murderers is truly remarkable," especially in contrast to all subsequent deaths in the play. As the first scene to exclude Richard, and the only scene to contain prose, this episode of Clarence's death is "remarkably inefficient" (Lopez, 2005, 299). In his extended dream Clarence recounts escaping the tower and sailing to Burgundy; on the ship Clarence imagines that his brother "from my cabin tempted me to walk / Upon the hatches" (1.4.12–13). The verb "tempted" anticipates Richard's devilish role in murdering Clarence, even as Clarence continues to have faith in his brother. Falling into the ocean Clarence narrates:

> O Lord, methought what pain it was to drown,
> What dreadful noise of water in mine ears,
> What sights of ugly death within mine eyes.
> Methoughts I saw a thousand fearful wracks,
> A thousand men that fishes gnawed upon,
> Wedges of gold, great anchors, heaps of pearl,
> Inestimable stones, unvalued jewels,
> All scattered in the bottom of the sea.
> Some lay in dead men's skulls, and in the holes
> Where eyes did once inhabit, there were crept—
> As 'twere in scorn of eyes—reflecting gems,
> That wooed the slimy bottom of the deep
> And mocked the dead bones that lay scattered by.
>
> (1.4.21–33)

These lines offer, in characteristically Shakespearean fashion, dazzling lyrical beauty precisely at a moment of pain or trauma. We pause here, anticipating death, to admire the lush riches contained within "dead men's skulls"—the "inestimable stones, unvalued jewels," that are lodged in eye sockets. A scene of "fearful wrecks," gnawing fishes, and dead bones is juxtaposed with the wealth of "reflecting gems," "Wedges of gold," and "heaps of pearl." We might read these images as signs of dazzling wealth, a nod to the ambitions of Richard who seeks the jeweled crown. But the oppositions of skulls and mud to the gems also evokes a broader religious discourse in the play, the opposition of body to soul, earth to heaven. These "unvalued" jewels are beyond price, the pure soul that stands eternal, beyond and within the mortal body. The scene is at once a reminder of the play's Christian setting, in which earthly power is temporal and inconsequential in comparison to the eternal, heavenly realm; and a reminder of the corruption in Richard's England, as men compromise their eternal salvation for earthly advancement.

Clarence's dream predicts his death, and the killer, Richard. But immediately following this dream comes one of the play's funnier exchanges, as the murderers argue about whether to kill Clarence. They are bumblers, concerned it might be cowardly to kill a sleeping man: "What, shall we stab him as he sleeps?" "No. He'll say 'twas done cowardly, when he wakes" (1.4.100–1). These men hesitate to kill because of a masculinist code about a fair fight, and perhaps also for fear of Clarence's testimony against them in the afterlife. As the men continue to linger, thinking on Judgment Day, the one claims he has a kind of remorse: "The urging of that word 'Judgement' hath bred a kind of remorse in me" (106–7). He hopes his "passionate humour . . . will change," thinking it will be better if he counts to twenty: "It was wont to hold me but while one tells twenty" (118–19). The opposition of timeless Heaven with these counting murderers, hoping to accomplish their damning mission, provokes laughs, further amplified when the memory of reward banishes conscience: "Remember our reward when the deed's done," says the first murderer, and the second responds, "Zounds, he dies! I had forgot the reward" (124–5). These murderers treat conscience like indigestion— something that's bothersome for a second and might go away: "'Where's thy conscience now?' / 'O, in the Duke of Gloucester's purse'" (126–7). We laugh—and in laughing we move to a comic register, away from Clarence and his dream, only to be brought back in the plaintive one-hundred line exchange between the murderers and the Duke. The scene ends with Clarence's death, immediately condemned by the second murderer: "A bloody deed, and desperately dispatched. / How fain, like Pilate, would I wash my hands / Of this most grievous murder" (270–2).

This episode with Clarence introduces a dynamic present in other scenes of dreams and prophecies: the play offers an invocation of a dream or curse or prophecy that is both very serious and also mocked. But notably the scene with Clarence ends on the godly realm, with an awareness of life beyond material circumstances: the conscience and repentance felt by the unnamed second murderer. This scene thus importantly offsets Richard's own Machiavellian vantage point in the play. Cutting this debate between the murderers, as is often done in adaptations of the play that struggle with its length, therefore cuts the audience's punctuated awareness of this metaphysical realm. Scholar Hugh Richmond argues that such cuts often cause "loss of psychological subtlety and of moral refinement." And the most "typical of these is the editing-out of the bizarre but highly significant debate between Clarence's murderers over the sleeping duke, which vividly illuminates the issues of legal authority and moral responsibility relevant to all the political assassinations and executions in the play" (Richmond, 1989, 61).

The princes: Repetition with a difference

So far we have been toggling between Richard and his opponents, exploring how Shakespeare alters his sources to increase our intimacy with Richard, even against our better judgment. Further, as I suggested earlier in the chapter, the repetition of murder hardens us to its effects, further increasing our improbable alliance with the villainous king. Yet there is, as poststructuralist theorist Gilles Deleuze writes, repetition with a difference. Arguably static, "reterritorializing" repetition, is purely mimetic, representing and reproducing what has come before. But "deterritorializing" repetition produces or highlights difference and is, as a result, transformative. Deleuze writes, "The first repetition is repetition of the Same, explained by the identity of the concept of representation; the second includes difference, and includes itself in the alterity of the Idea, in the heterogeneity of an 'a-presentation'" (Deleuze, 1994, 24). "Deterritorializing" repetition takes the original and alters it, reframing what had come before in a new light.

It is to such repetition with a difference that we now turn, namely to the death of the princes, the act that changes everything. Their murder follows the repetitious pattern: Richard states he wants them dead, he commissions their murder, and it occurs. We again have women lamenting the death in formalistic language. What tips the balance away from Richard? We might immediately answer that it is the audience's horror at the killing of children. But it is worth examining the play's language to see how it constructs this tipping point. After all, we do not see the murder of the children first-hand. It is instead the *structure* of their deaths that helps us understand the gravity of this act.

Shakespeare introduces two methods to distance the audience from Richard at this point. First, he depicts villains hesitating, and second, he reports the deaths third-hand. In the first case, in handling the princes' murders, the action that secured Richard's infamy, Shakespeare increases the moment's drama through Buckingham's hesitancy: the man who has supported and even ingeniously encouraged Richard's corrupt ambition now balks. Richard queries, "Ah, Buckingham, now do I play the touch / To try if thou be current gold indeed: / Young Edward lives. Think now what I would speak" (4.2.8–10), to which Buckingham responds, "Say on, my loving lord" (11). His density, in not naming the unnamable act, betrays his reluctance. Richard must demand, "Cousin, thou wast not wont to be so dull. / Shall I be plain? I wish the bastards dead" (4.2.17–18). When Richard asks directly, "Say, have I thy consent that they shall die?" he responds, "Give me some little breath, some pause, dear lord, / Before I positively speak in this" (23–5). This reluctance on the part of a very biased and invested courtier betrays the ethical horror of Richard's plan. Even those with blood on their hands and something to gain find the proposal abhorrent.

Catesby, incidentally, hesitates in precisely the same way about the death of Anne later in the scene. When Richard demands, "Rumour it abroad / That Anne my wife is grievous sick" (4.2.50–1), we learn Catesby's nonverbal response in

Richard's comment: "Look how thou dream'st! I say again, give out / That Anne my queen is sick and like to die" (4.2.56–7). In both of these quotations the embedded response of the listener codes the reluctance—for both Catesby and Buckingham, Richard has gone too far. Richard remarks "look how thou dream'st" of Catesby—a kind of stage direction that lets us know that Catesby can't believe what he's hearing; he looks befuddled. And similarly with Buckingham, Richard calls him "dull," accusing him of failing to get the point. But we understand what Richard does not: Buckingham knows what Richard implies, but he can't believe what he's hearing. They can't believe it because Richard has achieved his goal: he's king. So why does he need to kill his wife and nephews? Richard imagines that he stands on "brittle glass" without the marriage to Elizabeth and the death of the princes. He seeks to secure his throne, but in the process he pushes his allies too far, finding himself undermined and isolated instead.

We can hear the effect of this structure—Richard asking, recipients balking—when we compare it to Shakespeare's source in Holinshed's *Chronicles*. In one of the most dramatic moments in Holinshed, the historian recounts Richard's decision to dispatch his two nephews, who stand in his way to the crown:

> King Richard after his coronation, taking his way to Gloucester to visit (in his new honour) the town of which he bare the name of his old, devised (as he rode) to fulfill the thing which he before had intended. And forsomuch as his mind gave him, that his nephews living, men would not reckon that he could have right to the realm: he thought therefore without delay to rid them, as though the killing of his kinsmen could amend his cause, and make him a kindly king. Whereupon he sent one John Greene, (whom he specially trusted) unto sir Robert Brakenbury, constable of the Tower, with a letter and credence also, that the same sir Robert should in any wise put the two children to death.

(Holinshed, 1587)

Here, Holinshed deploys irony and sarcasm to suggest his own distance from Richard's murderous thoughts. In his phrase, "as though the killing of his kinsmen could amend his cause, and make him a kindly king," Holinshed offers his form of commentary, namely, murder will make Richard anything but "a kindly king." But the implied consent of Greene and Brakenbury establishes a community of murderers or guilty parties. Shakespeare's Richard is, by contrast, isolated in his desire (remember our list of thriller's attributes, among them the protagonist's fear). And Shakespeare reveals this potently in his handling of the murders.

It is a truism to say that first-hand accounts are more powerful than diluted ones told at a distance. So, turning to Shakespeare's second technique in creating distance from Richard, we might ask, why would he place us at a third or fourth remove from the play's, and history's, most notorious villainy, the murder of the princes? Richard commissions Tyrell who suborns Dighton and Forrest to undertake the murders; when we hear about the death, we hear Tyrell narrate the emotional response of others. Rather than diluting the experience, however, this distance amplifies it—we effectively hear of the singular responses of multiple audiences to this notorious act.

Tyrell, a man described as "discontented" and "haughty" (4.2.36–7) and vulnerable to "corrupting gold" (34), transforms into a classical messenger reporting the tragedy through soliloquy:

> The tyrannous and bloody act is done,
> The most arch deed of piteous massacre
> That ever yet this land was guilty of.
> Dighton and Forrest, who I did suborn
> To do this piece of ruthful butchery,
> Albeit they were fleshed villains, bloody dogs,
> Melted with tenderness and kind compassion,
> Wept like to children in their deaths' sad story.
> 'Oh, thus' quoth Dighton, 'lay the gentle babes.'
> 'Thus, thus,' quoth Forrest, 'girdling one another

Within their alabaster innocent arms.
Their lips were four red roses on a stalk,
And in their summer beauty kissed each other.
A book of prayers on their pillow lay,
Which once,' quoth Forrest, 'almost changed my mind.
But O, the Devil—' There the villain stopped;
When Dighton thus told on: 'We smothered
The most replenished sweet work of nature,
That from the prime creation e'er she framed.'
Hence both are gone with conscience and remorse;
They could not speak; and so I left them both,
To bear this tidings to the bloody King.

(4.3.1–22)

The murderers, whom the greedy Tyrell describes as "fleshed villains, bloody dogs," are horrified by their own act; Tyrell himself is chastened and mournful. As Dighton and Forrest become "children" themselves, weeping to tell the tale, the descriptor "bloody" shifts from the murderers to Richard, the "bloody king" Tyrell invokes at the speech's end. Forrest—as reported by Tyrell—offers some of the most moving lines in the play, in his image of the children entwined in each other's arms, lips like roses touching as they innocently sleep. He finds himself unable to narrate what he has done, breaking off as he attempts to recount his own failure to change his mind: "'But O, the Devil'—There the villain stopped." Dighton takes up the rest of the narration, and both men leave "with conscience and remorse," unable to speak further. The fact that their lines have been memorized and recounted by Tyrell amplifies their power; Forrest and Dighton's images stay with Tyrell, haunting him, as traumatized men now form a lament together, echoing the female voices in the play.

Tyrell's speech shifts our vantage point away from Richard. We feel the horror of these deaths because we realize that, in recounting them, even hardened criminals weep. Now when Richard enters the room, we are at a significant distance from him, intimate instead with Tyrrel:

KING RICHARD
Kind Tyrrel, am I happy in thy news?
TYRREL
If to have done the thing you gave in charge
Beget your happiness, be happy then,
For it is done.
KING RICHARD
But didst thou see them dead?
TYRREL
I did, my lord.

(4.3.24–8)

Richard's word "kind"—"kind Tyrell"—might remind us of Hamlet's famous "more than kin and less than kind," in which he puns on the word to illuminate the dissimilarity of Claudius from himself. Here, Richard deploys "kind" in an opposite fashion, to indicate not distance from but allegiance to Tyrell. Since "kind" signals at once sympathy (kindness) and likeness (of the same kind), to address Tyrell as "kind" rings perversely: a man Richard imagines to be a greedy murderer is, he reasons, like himself, ambitious and heartless; he is also, Richard posits, "kind" for successfully committing the requested act. But we now hear otherwise: the caricatured murderer shows the conscience and remorse this tyrannous king lacks. The repetition of the word "happy" draws further attention to Richard's jarring and inappropriate response. Tyrell repeats the word in a kind of disbelief, questioning that murder could lead to happiness, and thus further increasing the gap between Richard and his audiences both on and off stage.

Women

This tipping point away from Richard has an important effect: the secondary characters we might have dismissed earlier now take center stage, at least emotionally. Whereas Margaret had been derided in the earlier scene of her prophetic speech as a mad woman ranting at a condemning audience, with the princes' deaths, three women (Queen Elizabeth, Queen Margaret and the Duchess of York) come forward to speak in unison as mourners. In doing so they draw us in with their heightened emotion and formal rhetoric, two features of speech that arguably pushed us away earlier. Queen Margaret laments, "I had an Edward, till a Richard killed him; / I had a husband, till a Richard killed him" (4.4.40–1), and the Duchess of York responds, "I had a Richard too, and thou didst kill him; / I had a Rutland too; thou holp'st to kill him" (4.4.44–5). These lines of mirroring earlier signaled the inauthenticity of Richard's wooing: remember, he and Anne practiced such repetition. Further, the wrangling between Yorkist courtiers kept us at an emotional distance, making it hard to sympathize with any one figure. But now repetition helps contain what is otherwise inexpressible grief, and as the scene continues, Queen Elizabeth seeks Margaret's help in learning to curse. The houses of Lancaster and York come together in shared sorrow.

As the Duchess of York and Elizabeth take up Margaret's role as powerless, cursing prophets, the Duchess tells her new ally, "be not tongue-tied. Go with me, / And in the breath of bitter words let's smother / My damned son, which thy two sweet sons smothered" (4.4.132–4). Where earlier these women wrangled against each other they now come together against the tyrannical Richard, functioning, as Downie puts it, as a kind of chorus: "three women who have carried the emotional weight of events and whose suffering now gives them the right to function as a kind of moral chorus" (Downie, 1994, 137). To Downie, these women recalled "refugees," such as "women in black wandering round Europe after the last war" (Downie, 1994, 137). What is arguably a very difficult and non-naturalistic scene of mourning becomes a scene of sympathy and allegiance. After all why, now, does Margaret stop to speak to her opponents and join their lament? Downie finds an answer in the community of women: "in a sense she is elevated by her grief and by her satisfaction that, incredibly, all the things she predicted have come to pass" (Downie, 1994, 137).

In coming together against Richard, the play's women become, surprisingly, powerful. They ultimately compromise him as no other characters manage to do. Richard repeatedly imagines that he can manipulate women, only to find himself shocked by betrayal and condemnation where he expected— even in the face of his own villainy—love. His exchange with his mother in their final scene is an example of this. Anton Lesser, who played Richard III at the RSC, credits the exchange with his mother as the tipping point in Richard's fall. From the moment he gets the throne, Lesser suggests,

> Richard is losing power. An important part of this process is the confrontation with his mother (IV.iv) who "intercepts" him in his "expedition" against Buckingham's rebellion. God knows what the relationship between Richard and his mother has been like; clearly the conduit which should allow love to flow naturally between mother and child got bunged-up somewhere, and for Richard it seems it never operated at all. From his emergence from the womb the see-saw effect of alienation and defence, attack and self-protection, created a thick wall of isolation from his mother, driving him towards the superficial comradeship of his brothers, their roles as warriors bringing them into spurious unity as a "pack," though not to any real sort of love.
>
> (Lesser, 1994, 153)

If Richard condemns women, he also relies on them for his rise, for political marriage primarily, but also for a kind of acceptance. Yet he is denied such love. Thus, as Lesser puts it, "when she [Duchess of York] curses him she is expressing that absolute need to speak which we see several characters in the play confronting at certain points. She needs to express her horror at what she has given birth to, to crystallize it, to make it terminal" (Lesser, 1994, 154).

Shakespeare structures this late scene so that Richard turns from this rejection, offered by his mother, to Queen Elizabeth. He imagines that she will show him the affection and compliance he sought and failed to receive from his mother. He attempts to cajole her into supporting his marriage to her daughter, and she seems to comply, thereby fulfilling his political and emotional request. But he ends the scene not giddy at his success, as he had been with Anne, but instead bitter: he dismisses her as a "relenting fool, and shallow, changing woman" (4.4.431), condemning her for taking up his cause. He has expressed such misogyny before, and we may have even laughed with him against our better judgment. But at this stage he does not seem to recognize what the audience knows: Elizabeth placates him but has no intention of doing what he wants. Her daughter will marry Richmond. (Of course, not all interpreters of the play read her this way. Director William Alexander has another take, imagining that Richard won Elizabeth around "because he has a brilliant instinctive understanding of psychology . . . Richard understands her fundamental materialism. . .. Richard is saying to her, 'Look love, I can turn your tears into jewelry.' This gives the scene a much more disturbing quality" [Sher, 2006, 195].) But to many directors, actors, and readers, Elizabeth instead appears to have developed the cunning that Richard practices from the start: she deceives her onstage audience while preserving herself and her daughter for a more auspicious future, with the godly Richmond, soon to be King Henry VII.

Richmond

From an historical vantage point, Richmond is the culmination of the entire cycle initiated with the deposition of King Richard II, and chronicled by Shakespeare in his two tetralogies. Yet while Henry VII is historically grand—the founder of the Tudor dynasty and grandfather to Queen Elizabeth—from a theatrical vantage point, Richmond is hardly a character at all. He is the *deux ex machina*, a figure who appears at the eleventh hour to tie up the plot and end on a triumphant note. Martine Van Elk helps summarize the dilemma facing us as we analyze this character:

How, finally, does Richmond fit in? Does he represent an individual in control of his own destiny, a more effective king? Is he a pawn in a divine plan for England? While on the face of it, Richmond seems to fulfill God's plan with a heroic masculinity to match, combining contradictory Christian and warrior mentalities, few critics are now content to read him as a positive replacement for Richard. With King James's speech as well as the *Homily Against Disobedience* in mind, students appreciate the ideological obstacles Richmond has to overcome in order not to be seen as a satanic rebel. William Carroll claims that Richmond ironically gets away with seizing the crown rather than going through the more legitimate channels of succession by offering to reestablish order and ritual (1992). E. Pearlman appears to voice a consensus when he remarks, "Richmond's thoroughly conventional language is disciplined, ordered, measured, and drab. It demonstrates competence but lacks charisma and inspires loyalty but not love" (Pearlman, 1992, 59). Barbara Hodgdon's view of Richmond hinges on both a providential and a secular reading, as she calls him an "ideological function," whose word choices so resemble his enemy's that we find that "replacing a false tyrant with a true king simply exchanges one fiction for another, each marked by the same rhetorical mask."

(Van Elk, 2007, 12)

What Van Elk chronicles, the lack of depth to Richmond's character, might be a political necessity. He is, after all, invading the kingdom from a foreign shore, and toppling the sitting king. By most definitions this makes him a traitor. Shakespeare's structure helps to sidestep meditation on this problem by offering Richmond more as a symbol than a man with individual desires or ambitions. He represents law, order, ethics, stability, and salvation; what he *is*, as a human being with his own material longings, is beside the point. And this may be more broadly the case with monarchical rule. The symbolic, theological role of a monarch overtakes his or her individual body, a process represented in the Netflix series *The Crown*, which depicts how Elizabeth Windsor cedes to Gloriana.

Richmond affirms the forms of law in contrast to Richard, thereby increasing his apparent legitimacy:

> Richmond . . . is careful to observe the ceremonious and the traditional, from his planned marriage to Elizabeth through his prayer before the battle, to his oration to his troops. His final speech in the play brings together explicit ritual and the "form of law" generally. . . . Each line of this speech invokes a different ritual or principle of order: the decorum of funeral rites; the royal pardon; the subject's obedience of hierarchical authority; the ritual of the "sacrament"; and the union of opposites. Richmond says all the right things that could be said.
>
> (Carroll, 1992, 210–11)

This emphasis on law and ritual helps secure Richmond as a legitimate ruler. He seeks the crown not for himself, but for a set of principles. Furthermore, he appears to represent the play's murdered characters, those prophets and dreamers felled by Richard. Through prophetic language these characters seek the aid of a higher power, and such a power appears to arrive, now, in the form of Richmond. Thus even as Richmond on one level appears out of nowhere, a divine intervention with whom we have no contact before his grand entrance in the final act, he is also the culmination of an argument that the play makes throughout, on the presence of the divine, and the power of prophecy as this chapter has already explored. He is precisely the figure of retribution, promised by Queen Margaret.

It is in the dream sequence, and at the battle of Bosworth Field, that the play's providential argument comes into its full ascendancy. First, all the murdered characters come forward and curse Richard, while praising Richmond. The argument for Richmond wins the day, and Richard's mocking of prophetic language comes back to haunt him. This sequence is the climax of all the dreams and prophecies and curses we have traced so far:

> *Enter the* GHOSTS *of the two young Princes*
> GHOSTS [of Princes] [*to Richard*]
>   Dream on thy cousins smothered in the Tower.
>   Let us be lead within thy bosom, Richard,
>   And weigh thee down to ruin, shame, and death.
>   Thy nephews' souls bid thee despair and die.
>   [*to Richmond*] Sleep, Richmond, sleep in peace and wake
>   in joy;
>   Good angels guard thee from the boar's annoy.
>   Live, and beget a happy race of kings;
>   Edward's unhappy sons do bid thee flourish.
>
> (5.3.146–53)

These figures are haunting England, seeking reparation. The scene's symmetry mirrors the structure of the play itself, a play constructed through repetition and rhetorical order in the face of chaos. The scene also mirrors, on what critics call a metatheatrical level, the condition of theater within the play itself. Metatheater refers to aspects of a play that draw our direct attention to the theater itself—most obviously through the staging of a play within a play, as in *Hamlet;* but also through characters who take on multiple roles, like Richard; or through, in this scene, the appearance of the ghosts. Each of these figures has been laid to rest by Richard, but now as they reappear, they assert the skill of theater for the other side. If Richard has been the one successfully manipulating roles and parts until the play's fifth act, other characters now take on unexpected parts, even to the point of coming alive again, an argument Stephen Marche makes:

the dead return in a theatrical procession to tell their stories exactly and with precision. When the metatheatrical dimensions of this triumph are considered, it would seem at first to be redemptive for the theatrical project: whereas before theatricality itself was damned as a means by which historical truth was perverted, here theatre is the very agent of its triumph.

(Marche, 2003, 52)

This scene offers a commentary, Marche argues, on the nature of theater itself within the play: initially Richard uses role playing for his own villainous purposes, but the procession of ghosts instead asserts theater's power for good—in the form of bringing the dead to life through scripted lines, each echoing the one before.

Yet even as this is a key scene in Shakespeare's rendition of events—indeed, a climactic scene—the staging of Act 5, scene 3 seems to be an issue for directors. Both the Olivier and the McKellen film versions choose not to have the ghosts go back and forth between Richard and Richmond. Instead, Olivier shows the ghosts as ethereal, watery images delivering a portion of the play's original lines to Richard, while cutting the parallel messages for Richmond. McKellen encounters voices tormenting him in his dream, a precursor to the awakened conscience. But these are not the lines of the ghosts but curses from earlier in the play. The loss of the scene's structure moving from Richard to Richmond, from "Despair and die" to "Live and flourish," undermines the scene's role as the culmination of the play's argument on providential history, training our attention on Richard's struggle alone. I invite you to watch these scenes, in Olivier and McKellen, and think about the effects of such revision and cutting. What does it accomplish and what is lost?

Richard's conscience

Equally surprisingly, one of the key speeches in the play— Richard waking up to his own conscience—gets cut in part or entirely from productions. Yet it is the climax of Richard's soliloquies, as he is alone with himself and, for the first time, afraid. What had been external voices condemning Richard— in the form of his mother, his wife, his Queen—become internalized, as he condemns and frightens himself. He wakes up crying,

> Give me another horse! Bind up my wounds!
> Have mercy, Jesu.—Soft, I did but dream.
> O coward conscience, how dost thou afflict me!
> The lights burn blue. It is now dead midnight.
> Cold fearful drops stand on my trembling flesh.
> What do I fear? Myself? There's none else by.
> Richard loves Richard, that is, I am I.
> Is there a murderer here? No. Yes, I am.
> Then fly! What, from myself? Great reason why?
> Lest I revenge. What, myself upon myself?
> Alack. I love myself. Wherefore? For any good
> That I myself have done unto myself?
> O, no. Alas, I rather hate myself
> For hateful deeds committed by myself.
> I am a villain. Yet I lie; I am not.
> Fool, of thyself speak well. Fool, do not flatter.
> My conscience hath a thousand several tongues,
> And every tongue brings in a several tale,
> And every tale condemns me for a villain.

(5.3.177–95)

Richard separates from himself, splitting into his villainous half and the part that condemns such villainy. Words like "fearful," "trembling," and "fly" are not ones we associate with Richard: he revels in action and danger, and mocks weak calls for "mercy," Jesus, and the claims of "conscience." Furthermore, the Richard we know to this point exhibits singularity of purpose: he is defined by his will power to such a degree he seems a Nietzschean Übermensch, or super man. He challenges Christian fantasy in favor of the inhabited world around him. Here he is instead a divided being, of "several tongues" which speak in discordant voices.

We already surveyed this speech in Chapter One's discussion of meter, where we noted its rhythmical variety. Richard speaks, uncharacteristically, in short sentences that stop in the middle of the line. The choppiness of the speech, we observed, betrays how emotion governs him, not reason. Through its irregularity of meter and enjambed lines, the speech seems to interrupt itself. Furthermore, the speech's rhetorical devices such as epistrophe create not a sense of order but of confusion and hysteria: the repetition of a word or phrase at the end of successive clauses, rather than at the beginning, can have—as it does here—the effect of doubling back, circling around an idea without resolving it. Richard's hold on his world is slipping as he begins to question himself and meditate on an afterlife he'd never considered.

This speech can be very difficult to pull off in performance. It is one of Richard's most famous and moving speeches, but it requires the actor to make believable a sharp contrast with his earlier character, a reversal of what scholar Hugh Richmond (1989) calls "Richard's initial dominance and flair." In the Colley Cibber version of the play, this dramatic shift of character is hardly felt because the villainy of Richard is so much more acute: "There is little cathartic shift in the audience's attitude to Richard, because he remains far more consistent in his attitude of bold wickedness" (Richmond, 1989, 51). Richmond hypothesizes that Richard Burbage must have managed this speech so well that Shakespeare returned to it, in expanded form, in his *Macbeth*: there, too, a hero moves from compelling ambition to overpowering anxiety. But later generations of actors instead performed Richard through the more manageable Cibber version, in which Garrick triumphed: "If the original scripts had been a vehicle for Burbage to achieve a distinct transmutation of affect, the new text served as a tidy frame within which to display the virtuosity in a merely criminal role of great actor-managers such as Garrick" (Richmond, 1989, 51). Even in the Cibber version, however, the strain of playing the ambitious Richard and this later, inward Richard is great enough that actors have been known for shining in one or the other parts. Thus in the 1750–51 theater season in London, "well-informed connoisseurs took to watching Barry for the first three acts [at Covent Garden] and then rushing to Drury Lane to catch the two final acts, in which Garrick shone" (Colley, 1992, 8).

For modern actors using the Shakespeare script, the shift in character and the awakening of conscience is daunting: how to communicate a distinctly different Richard in this final sequence, a man awakened to conscience? One way of playing the scene, which helps us to hear the distinct languages of the speech, is as a kind of dialogue: one actor, for example, played the speech as "a dialogue between two totally distinct voices, assigning alternating passages to them throughout the speech. On close analysis the interrogative syntax invites this dialectical treatment . . . the assignment of alternating passages elicited two consistent but contrasting personas, a hitherto dominant Ego and a newly surfacing Conscience, each fighting to seize control of Richard's definitive identity" (Richmond, 1989, 43–4). This speech—and the challenges of playing it—helps illuminate what critics have long seen as Shakespeare's characteristic ability, to stage a "multi-layered concept of personality, in which provocative yet plausible discontinuities become key to stage character, not labored consistency" (Richmond, 1989, 44). It is precisely because Shakespeare forms a character with depth—contrasting layers of personality—that actors find themselves wrestling between naturalism on the one hand, and psychological and even theological insight on the other.

My kingdom for a horse

The contrasts within the character of Richard are amplified by the figure of Richmond, a two-dimensional character who displays no such tangled depths. Instead, the invading hero wakes up on the morning of battle refreshed, reporting "The sweetest sleep and fairest-boding dreams / That ever entered in a drowsy head" (5.3.227–8). He is, he claims, "jocund" (232) in remembering this dream. Yet the gap between Richard's tormented night, and Richmond's restful one, is arguably undercut in their speeches to their troops. On one level, Richmond appears stable, assured, and self-possessed, while Richard offers a haunted, bloody speech. Yet Richmond's speech is seeped in precisely the imagery of violence that Richard deploys throughout the play, challenging the easy distinction between these warriors.

Thus as we move to the end of the play, and analyze these final speeches, I invite you to open your ears to the points of contact between what might appear quite distinct language spoken by these men. As Richmond turns to his troops after his night of restful sleep he tells them:

> God, and our good cause, fight upon our side.
> The prayers of holy saints and wronged souls,
> Like high-reared bulwarks, stand before our faces.
> Richard except, those whom we fight against
> Had rather have us win than him they follow.
> For, what is he they follow? Truly, gentlemen,
> A bloody tyrant and a homicide;
> One raised in blood, and one in blood established;
> One that made means to come by what he hath,
> And slaughtered those that were the means to help him;
> A base foul stone, made precious by the foil
> Of England's chair, where he is falsely set;
> One that hath ever been God's enemy.
> Then, if you fight against God's enemy,
> God will, in justice, ward you as His soldiers;
> If you do sweat to put a tyrant down,
> You sleep in peace, the tyrant being slain;

(5.3.240–56)

Richmond uses the language of tyranny to describe Richard and justify his fall: Richard is a stone, an enemy to God.

Richmond doesn't describe his own power, but instead God's: Richard will be toppled by an interventionist force of the divine. This is precisely the Tudor argument. Richmond is appointed by God and is not seeking the crown for his own benefit but for the nation's. But careful study of Richmond's language might leave us uneasy about his claims. First, as Richard P. Wheeler argues, if Richmond promises perpetual peace and concord, in doing so he "must take over a rhetoric that has already been colored by the sardonic humor of Richard and the prolonged laments of his victims. Richmond's person simply does not carry enough force to jolt his key terms free from associations that have accrued to them in the course of the previous four acts" (Wheeler, 1971–2, 307). For example, the word "peace" appears as if in quotation marks throughout the play: the "weak, piping time of peace" (1.1.24) opens the play, a prelude to Richard's murderous designs; King Edward's attempt to establish "peace" with his court throughout Act 2, Scene 1 (5, 6, 44, 51) is overshadowed by our awareness of Clarence's death; Richard embraces "peace" on Edward's death, seeking the crown by executing Hastings to preserve the "peace of England" (3.5.45). For Richmond to end the play invoking peace might make the audience more wary than secure.

If Richmond's terms are sullied by Richard's ironic use of them earlier in the play, we might also notice how Richmond relies on the same oppositional logic, tinged with violence and ambition for the crown, with which Richard began: lovers and villains, peace and war, sun and clouds. Joel Slotkin helps illuminate what is at stake in this speech, and Richmond's mode of address more generally, when he writes:

Richmond's speeches consistently alternate images of England at peace, grateful wives, and mingled red and white roses with gory descriptions of Richard, sons butchering their fathers, and rivers of bloody tears. Rather than eliminating the sinister, Richmond seems to be trying to subordinate it to the beautiful in the service of a moral goal—to perform the reverse of Richard's grotesque juxtapositions. The admirable effort to achieve aesthetic balance could represent a poetic solution to the problem of the sinister if it were more successful. But critics differ widely on the effectiveness of Richmond's speeches, and many of his most powerful moments rely primarily on the same sinister imagery that gives Richard's speeches their poetic force.

(Slotkin, 2007, 24)

Indeed, Richmond's lines on Richard as a "base foul stone" falsely set in "England's chair," a king who is "raised in blood" and "in blood established," offer the kind of incendiary rhetoric deployed in the twentieth century by politicians like Enoch Powell in his infamous "Rivers of Blood" speech, figuring a modern England under threat from without and within. Richmond offers such a denunciation in his image of a foul and invading Richard covered in blood, even as he, Richmond, is the one invading England and felling its subjects in battle.

Richard, of course, offers an equally incendiary and nationalist argument against invading foreigners. As a result the distinction between Richmond and Richard is not as great as Tudor historiography, and the play's argument on prophetic interventions, might have us think. Richard tells his troops,

What shall I say more than I have inferred?
Remember whom you are to cope withal,
A sort of vagabonds, rascals and runaways,
A scum of Bretons and base lackey peasants,
Whom their o'ercloyed country vomits forth
To desperate adventures and assured destruction.
You sleeping safe, they bring to you unrest;
You having lands and blest with beauteous wives,
They would restrain the one, distain the other.

(5.3.314–22)

Richard's English nationalistic language casts the invaders as a "scum of Bretons," led by Richmond, a "milksop" (325) and a foreigner coming to England as a form of pestilence or vomit. Even as we realize how desperate this speech is, it's also powerful in its theatrical effects. It is precisely a call to arms based in opposition and hatred that can unify troops under an authoritarian ruler. In this speech Richard continues to defy the odds, appearing even at the moment of his hysterical tyranny as a potential hero. Furthermore, his language continues to surprise us. Re-read Richmond's speech to his troops against Richard's. What images stand out to you? Richmond gives us the potent image of the stone. But Richard offers more startling, less familiar, images: a country vomiting forth its undesirables; a weakling whose feet have never even felt cold in the snow; a group of rats too poor to hang themselves. These images are—as we've seen throughout— both inventive and funny. His final line in this call to arms— "Amaze the welkin with your broken staves" (341)—is especially gripping. One nineteenth-century critic called it "extravagant, ridiculous in the highest degree" (Becket, 1815, 123). What does it mean? At the last, Richard imagines amazing—bewildering or astonishing—heaven itself. Welkin can mean a cloud but also, as here, the sky, firmament, or vault of heaven. With this final cry he goes into battle proving himself to be a tireless fighter, relentless in his power, and unwilling to surrender.

But what of this famous line, "a horse, a horse, my kingdom for a horse!" (5.4.7)? We're finally here, turning to the one line you probably knew before reading the play. Why does it stand out? First, it encapsulates Richard's character. It is a line filled with Richard's grit and determination to continue fighting, willing to trade the very kingdom he commanded for a mere horse, in order to keep fighting. If such a trade seems hyperbolic or figurative, recent research into Richard's frame indeed supports this notion of Richard's dependency upon his horse. In a documentary chronicling the exhumation and analysis of Richard's body, *Secrets of the Dead: Resurrecting Richard III*, scientists and historians study the precise nature of the king's physical frame. Then, commissioning a living body double for

Richard, they shape a medieval suit of armor and saddle for him to test how he might have fared in war. They discover, surprisingly, that for a man with a spine pitched at 80 degrees, the accouterments of medieval warfare would have aided him: the heavy armor and unyielding wooden saddle would have stabilized his spine, allowing him greater power than he would have on foot in battle. Hence the importance of his horse—it helped to level the playing field. The play's famous line, which could be read as extravagant enough to be funny, thus has a ring of historical truth. Commenting on the number of injuries that the historical Richard sustained in battle as evidenced by the skull factures on the discovered skeleton, Jonathan Slinger notes,

> it's interesting to find out how many injuries the real Richard sustained . . . Presumably he must have come off his horse. Again, Shakespeare seems to have been right about that: one of the most famous scenes he ever wrote is Richard staggering around yelling: "A horse, a horse! My kingdom for a horse!" I love the idea that he didn't imagine that moment.

> ("Richard III: Shakespearean Actors . . .," 2013)

Staging this final battle is one of the joys and challenges of any production of *Richard III*. Is it an athletic encounter between Richard and his foe? Or is it instead a form of psychological warfare, as the newly awakened conscience of Richard undermines his efforts on the field? Having mocked dreams, Richard now is felled by one; having dismissed prophecies, they now haunt him and arguably—at least as Anton Lesser performed it—topple him even more powerfully than Richmond's sword:

> We decided to stage the battle so that the audience might think that perhaps Richard was going to win, that Richmond was about to get it. We devised the final fight to show Richard about to kill Richmond until some of the ghosts returned to utter 'Despair and die.' They stopped him in the

course of his succeeding and that was when he was seen to be completely drained of his power. In a sense the moment suggested a supernatural intervention, though it could be interpreted as the audience wished: have the ghosts actually appeared to him on the battlefield or are they a metaphor for the awakening of conscience.

(Lesser, 1994, 158)

For other readers and directors, the final scene reveals Richard's renewed commitment to the fight, his prick of conscience banished in favor of his lance. As Olivier stages it, Richard is so strong in battle he's felled only by a gang of Richmond's warriors descending on him from every direction.

The play ends with Richmond's gesture toward the Tudor house, the reigning queen Elizabeth on the throne:

And then, as we have ta'en the sacrament,
We will unite the white rose and the red.
. . .
O, now let Richmond and Elizabeth,
The true succeeders of each royal house,
By God's fair ordinance conjoin together;
And let their heirs, God, if Thy will be so,
Enrich the time to come with smooth-faced peace,
With smiling plenty and fair prosperous days.
. . .
Now civil wounds are stopped; peace lives again.
That she may long live here, God say amen.

(5.5.18–41)

Richmond speaks here of his ascendency. What might strike you, though, is that he does so in the third person. Read his lines again, from "O, now let Richmond and Elizabeth. . ." But this time imagine that the speech is offered by the figure of the Chorus or as epilogue, as in the case of Marlowe's *Doctor Faustus* or Shakespeare's *As You Like It*. What difference does it make, to hear Richmond offer prediction and prayer for himself, rather than to hear these lines spoken by someone else?

In a volume concentrated on words, it makes sense to pay particular attention to the play's final one: "amen." Offered at the end of Richmond's prayer for a peaceful England, this word may seem formulaic and unremarkable. But Ramie Targoff teases out the word's complex appearance in the play since, as she notes, the play stages not one but two successions to the throne, both occasions asking an audience to join in "amen" to end the ceremony. She writes,

> Although the circumstances of these two instances are very different—the first involves the fraudulent "election" of Gloucester, the second, the crowning of the worthy and victorious Richmond—both scenes strikingly, and perhaps unsettlingly, depend for their resolution upon a collective response of "amen." And if in the first instance, this response, however contrived, ultimately succeeds, in the second instance, "amen" lingers on the stage unanswered ... For Henry VII's right to the throne to be validated within the play's construction of kingly election, Shakespeare would seem somewhat daringly to require an unscripted, voluntary gesture of either theatrical or devotional assent from the audience: the clapping of hands or the utterance of "amen."
>
> (Targoff, 2002, 64–5)

Richmond's final word thus demands, for its success, our own participation in the event. Having spent a play enticed and taunted by a usurping king who invites us to join him, our relationship to such metatheater has arguably been tried to the breaking point. As in the case of Richmond's speeches analyzed above, here his words eerily echo Richard's own, compromising the effects of his attempted closure with its presumed moral as well as military victory. In this final speech, one might argue that Shakespeare fails to secure the Tudor legacy as neatly as Hall, Holinshed, and More had done before him. But that is a question I will leave up to you to decide for yourselves, using the skills of close reading we've developed so far in this book.

Writing matters

Dreams

Find the dreams and prophecies that seem fantastical—such as Margaret's long list of curses, or Clarence's or Stanley's dream—and consider how they prove true, developing an argument about the play's broader relationship to prophecy.

You might also like to consider an historical twist in developing this assignment: Shakespeare's play both invites us to dismiss Margaret, and reveals the truth of her claims; in an incredible twenty-first century parallel, the screenwriter Philippa Langley "prophesized" the location of Richard's body, and endured skepticism and ridicule for her claims. She had to raise most of the funds for the excavation of the presumed site herself—and even after archaeologists dug up a body, she found herself mocked by the general public. But DNA testing confirmed that her hunches were indeed correct: she'd discovered Richard III's remains, under car park asphalt in Leicester. How might Shakespeare's portrait of Margaret resonate with modern examples of condemned, but ultimately correct, prophets?

Gender

Consider gender disparities and stereotypes in the play, both as offered through Richard's opinions of women and through the female characters' actions and language.

Sometimes women interact with Richard independently (Richard and Anne), and at other points women act as a chorus commenting on events. How does Richard view these forms of female speech? Is he alone in his view—is he exceptional—or is he in concert with others? Considering that Richard voices some misogynist tropes (women should be silent, chaste, and obedient) is Shakespeare critiquing such attitudes to women by putting them in the mouth of Richard?

History

This is a play based in history, but drawn from chronicles that are themselves biased against Richard. How does this play measure up as a history? Or how does it draw attention to itself as an imaginative and even tragic work, rather than one of history?

Here you might consider the role of prophecy and the supernatural in the play. Does the prophetic language participate in the play's imaginative effects, or is it in the service of the play's historical message? How might the supernatural realm appear opposed to historical fact, or how might it be intimately tied to history?

CHAPTER THREE

Language Through Time

The reign of King Richard III, from the first moment of its chronicling under Henry VII, has served as a commentary on political rulership. That commentary extends, as previous chapters have traced, from Polydore Vergil through Thomas More, Raphael Holinshed, and Edward Hall up to, according to some, Shakespeare. These historical accounts chronicle Richard's tyranny in order to support the rise of Henry VII. The story of Richard III thus aids, as we've already explored in our discussion of the Tudor myth of history, a specific political purpose. But the political uses of Richard, and particularly of Shakespeare's *King Richard III*, extend far beyond Tudor England. Indeed, many twentieth- and twenty-first-century productions take up the play's role as political commentary by shifting away from the Tudor rise to other moments in time. Shakespeare's play offers, to new generations of directors, a form of political allegory through which to narrate and explore the rise of tyranny in their own time.

This allegorical potential of the play, as critic Stephen Greenblatt writes in a 2016 *New York Times* commentary, lies in its exploration of a timely question: how could a great country end up being governed by a sociopath? Richard's villainy is evident to all; his vicious, bullying tendencies palpably clear. Yet his rise nevertheless occurs, despite its seeming impossibility. Richard thus stands, at least from Greenblatt's vantage point shortly before the 2016 American presidential election, as a cautionary tale on Donald Trump. From his theatricality to his improbable ascension, from his bitter grudges to his privileged background, Trump might well be a modern Richard. If so, Greenblatt argues, audiences (and voters) beware: for Shakespeare exposes how we, the audience, are "charmed again and again by the villain's jaunty outrageousness, by his indifference to the ordinary norms of human decency, by the lies that seem to be effective even though no one believes them, by the seductive power of sheer ugliness. Something in us enjoys every minute of his horrible ascent to power" (Greenblatt, 2016). Audiences are thus—like those enabling characters within *Richard III*, who prove unable or unwilling to resist—silent "like dumb statues or breathing stones." Greenblatt concludes his commentary with the following warning: "Shakespeare's words have an uncanny ability to reach out beyond their original time and place and to speak directly to us. We have long looked to him, in times of perplexity and risk, for the most fundamental human truths. So it is now. Do not think it cannot happen, and do not stay silent" (Greenblatt, 2016).

This chapter explores the uncanny ability of Shakespeare's words to reach beyond their original time and place. It does so by studying a range of adaptations of *Richard III* as political allegory, a process often realized through costuming and set design rather than any additions to the text. We find ourselves transported to 1930s fascist Europe, or 1960s mafia culture in New York City, or 2010 dictatorships in the Arab world, through gestures and military insignias, choices of weapons or physical swagger. Richard appears, in these productions, as Hitler or Mussolini, a mafia don, Saddam Hussein or Gaddafi. In exploring such allegorical adaptations, we will consider what it means to transport the play to such precise historical moments with little alteration to the text. Are the details of Richard's tyranny specific to his own reign? Or are they, as these productions suggest, generalizable to such an extent that Richard can stand for a modern dictator from any region of the globe? What are the implications of using *Richard III* to think through global historical traumas?

Beginnings

The process of adapting *Richard III* for a new era began with Colley Cibber's *Tragical History of King Richard III* (1699). This neoclassicizing version of the play, as noted in Chapter Two, trimmed down the plot. It also did away with the more prophetic elements of the text, from Margaret to the ghosts. If Cibber did not adapt the play for explicitly political purposes, in reframing it he initiated a long and continuing process of transforming *Richard III* to suit particular audiences. It is therefore worth our while to start with Cibber in exploring the process of adapting Shakespeare's villain.

Cibber's version of the play drew more attention to Richard, and focused less upon his effect on other characters. This re-emphasis was justified on dramatic grounds. As the eighteenth-century editor of Shakespeare, George Steevens, put it in his praise of Cibber's edition of the play,

> what modern audience would patiently listen to the narrative of Clarence's Dream, his subsequent expostulation with the murderers, the prattle of his children, the soliloquy of the Scrivener, the tedious dialogue of the citizens, the ravings of Margaret, the gross terms thrown out by the Duchess of York on Richard, the repeated progress to execution, the superfluous train of spectres, and other undramatick incumbrances.

> (Steevens, as cited in Siemon, 2009, 88)

Steevens's list suggests that non-Richardian moments of the play dampen the drama. Richard, he argues, is the main show, and other episodes detract from that simple but powerful structure. Of course, Steevens's list of detractions includes much of what we closely read in the last chapter. Indeed, some of the speeches he derides are, to my ear, among the play's most gripping, such as Clarence's dream and Margaret's prophecies. But the Cibber version of the play continues to influence modern versions, precisely by cutting the scene with Clarence and the figure of Queen Margaret on the grounds that they slow down the play's dramatic progress and confuse the plot.

In concentrating more directly on Richard, Cibber moved away from political-historical drama or morality tale to a more naturalized story. Cibber's is not the story of "history coming home to roost" (Siemon, 2009, 88). Instead, Cibber shaped a personal tragedy, eliminating divine elements of the play because, as Scott Colley argues, "The ghosts violate taste and propriety." He elaborates, writing, "critics, like many of the major actors, regard the play as Richard's personal tragedy and not as a providential drama of a nation's deliverance from tyranny" (Colley, 1992, 7). Colley's stage history of *Richard III* illuminates how "[i]n the theatre, few actors have wanted to contend for long with the invisible world. They have wanted to battle Richmond, not avenging angels . . . Cibber's decision to slight the invisible world thus has satisfied most Richards . . . Divine agents could diminish Richard's hold upon the audience which has been building during four full acts of gleeful, earthbound robustiousness" (Colley, 1992, 6–7).

The success of eighteenth-century actor David Garrick, who triumphed in the role and doubled Drury Lane house attendance in the process, amplifies these changes in emphasizing emotional insight over historical determinism. Garrick's Richard became a figure of "uncertainty, vulnerability, self-pity and pained self-awareness. From Cibber's final act, Garrick constructed a hero who dies grandly, and Richards would continue doing so even when translated back into Shakespeare's less supportive play" (Siemon, 2009, 90). Further, Garrick's "suffering protagonist suited period demands for 'sympathetic imagination' and emphasized 'fluctuations of mind.' Garrick conveyed that 'Kings themselves' by their 'sympathizing Souls . . . were *Men*, and *felt* like the rest of their Species'" (Siemon, 2009, 90–1). This pitiful and sympathetic Richard—the product not of Cibber's text alone, but of Garrick's powerful interpretation of it—arguably helped to encourage a sense of affiliation or kinship with Richard as a struggling soul. We are no longer horrified at

Richard, but instead drawn into sympathy with him, a morally problematic position. The great Romantic actor Edmund Kean, whose Richard dominated the stage in the early nineteenth century, continued to develop these complex identifications with Richard. Praised by William Hazlitt as "towering and lofty; equally impetuous and commanding; haughty, violent and subtle; bold and treacherous; confident in his strength as well as his cunning" (Siemon, 2009, 94–5), Kean's Richard—a romantic genius—had the power to draw in audiences against their own moral judgment.

One of Shakespeare's most talented interpreters was the classical actor Ira Aldridge, the first African American to tour the globe playing key Shakespeare roles, including Othello, Macbeth, Shylock, Lear, and Richard. Performing Richard in Cibber's rendition of the play, Aldridge's performances drew further attention to the character's interior life and motivations. One critic wrote—in comments resonant with the psychological rendition of Richard by Garrick—that Aldridge "made Richard more beautiful on stage, in order to focus more fully on the development of the character. He fully depicted [the King's] inner motivations, the nuances of his soul. Thus, his Richard . . . moves from inside out instead of outside in!" (Lindfors, 2013, 246). Another commentator wrote of his performance in Hungary that "Aldridge's Richard III was as new as it was touching. The highlights of our guest's performance lay in depicting the outburst of innate defiance in the middle of loving pretense and flattery; or in the raw, shocking *Schadenfreude* after he fooled someone; or the victory of his heroic nature over the stabs of conscience; or the sharp contrast between his real and his pretended character" (Lindfors, 2013, 114). Aldridge, like Garrick and Kean before him, developed Cibber's Richard by drawing attention to his character's complexity, revealing inner motivations and eliciting sympathy from the audience. The actors achieved this effect by expanding the possibilities of Cibber's script itself.

But Cibber's adaptation does diminish how deeply Shakespeare's original meditates on historical providence and determination. Cibber concentrates evil in Richard whereas Shakespeare "makes it apparent from the beginning that Richard's tragedy must be understood in the larger tragedy of a nation that has long been at civil war. By beginning the play with the murder of the king [Henry VI], Cibber personalizes the violence which in Shakespeare's tragedy had been a communal violence" (Colley, 1992, 22). Furthermore, in striving for clarity and balance, Cibber also simplified the struggles of Richard into what Norman Rabkin deems a rational battle between conscience and ambition. In Shakespeare, by contrast, the title character suffers from a kind of self-destruction that is not so neatly categorized:

> To his final breath [Cibber's] Richard is torn between mounting ambition and agonizing conscience; at the last he recognizes he has lost the fruits of both. The scheme is far more rational than Shakespeare's, not entertaining for a moment the possibility that the character is really motivated not by neat polarities but rather by the impulse to destruction and self-destruction that makes Shakespeare's Richard both painful to contemplate and human.
>
> (Rabkin, 1981, 101)

If Cibber's adaptation continues to influence directors, nevertheless a series of modern stage and film productions insist upon the play as a tragedy of a nation. Turning from the eighteenth century to a different interpretive moment—at the turn of the twenty-first—this chapter's next sections will examine how three other actors—Ian McKellen, Kevin Spacey, and Fayez Kazak—interpret the role. Specifically we will see how the Romantic portraits of Richard, illuminating sympathizing souls and inner motivations, cede to more directly political stagings of the king. Richard appears not as a tortured soul but as an ambitious and ruthless dictator, with Shakespeare's play offering a commentary on modern times. Notably moving Richards still persist, of course. And the audience continues to enjoy an intimacy with Richard—

particularly, in the three productions we explore below, as a result of the king's humor. These cunning, witty, and often funny Richards conscript us through laughter into intimacy and collusion. But this intimacy is not to be mistaken for sympathy; modern audiences are not expected to feel for Richard in the same way his nineteenth-century interpreters might have. Instead these three modern productions attest to a broad interest in how Shakespeare's language and plotting might offer a way of thinking through political crises. They use the play to warn against, or at least chart the rise of, fascism and tyranny. Such applications of the play neatly accord with the story's uses at the moment of its first productions by Vergil and More, suggesting an historical circularity to the fascination with this villainous character.

Fascist Richard

Ian McKellen's performances in the playhouse and on film offer an immediate (and viewable) example of Richard as political allegory. McKellen, who starred in The National Theatre's 1990 production of *Richard III*, directed by Simon Eyre, as well as in Richard Loncraine's film version based on this stage production, appears decked in the imagery and mannerisms of 1930s fascism. Here is Jami Roger's account of play: "Richard's takeover as king was visually signified by the familiar iconography of a totalitarian political rally, complete with a mob chanting 'Amen' in response to the declaration 'Long live King Richard, England's royal King!' Simultaneously, Richard was lifted above the crowd on a mechanical dais, raising his arm in a fascist salute as a banner bearing his insignia unfurled beneath" (Rogers, 2012, 99). Reviews of the production noted precisely this shift between the first and second half of the play: "Just before the interval, this Richard becomes Adolf Hitler in black shirt and jackboots . . . his arm taking unilateral action in a Nazi salute" (Osborne, 1990, 16). Director Simon Eyre seems well aware of this parallel:

according to Eyre's colleague on the set, designer Bob Crowley, Eyre "was very interested in an 'It could have happened here' idea, and he just drew very obvious parallels between Richard's rise to power and the fascist movement that was going on in England prior to the Second World War" (Rogers, 2012, 103). In the film version, Loncraine increases this iconography of European fascism by replacing the image of a boar inside of St. George's cross with a black boar in a circle of white, on a red banner—an image that immediately recalls Nazi flags.

But as Jami Rogers argues of this Simon Eyre stage production, the fascist staging of *Richard III* was not solely a commentary on 1930s Europe or even 1930s England. Instead the setting and iconography allowed the director to comment upon a particular, and very contemporary, version of English fascism during the time of its 1990s production. In the case of Eyre's production of Richard, he conceived of it in 1989, as the Berlin Wall and the dictatorship of Ceaucescu both fell, and as Thatcher continued to govern in England. Eyre comments, it "is astonishing the way in which the play lays out a blueprint for the rise of tyranny which every tyrant of the twentieth century appears to have followed" (Rogers, 2012, 102). To prove her point on the play's investigation not solely of 1930s fascism but also of 1990s tyranny, Rogers reads the play at the moment of its London run, during what she calls the "Fascism and its Consequences season." In this year, a range of plays, including Eyre's *Richard*, along with Joshua Sobol's *Ghetto*, Martin Sherman's *Bent* and several others, sought to interrogate threats of tyranny and totalitarianism.

Through this lens of political allegory, the nature of the audience's relationship to Richard shifts, as Peter S. Donaldson writes in comparing McKellen's Richard to other interpretations of the role earlier in the century: "as I read the film, Richard is not a star for us in the same way that, for example, Olivier was in the role or that Al Pacino strives to be in *Looking for Richard*. McKellen refuses the challenge of making the wooing scene a seduction of the screen audience as well as of Lady Anne, which Olivier responds to with virtuosity and charm and Pacino with obsessive and repeated attempts at sexual charisma" (Donaldson, 2002, 257). Watch these three productions and decide for yourself: Does McKellen strive to woo the audience, as arguably Pacino and Olivier do? Or does he distance us as he seduces Anne? Or do they instead seek to entrap us into unexpected intimacies, shocking us with ruthless villainy in the process? This is what McKellen's Richard achieves from the first speech, as he lures us into the men's bathroom with him while plotting Clarence's downfall (see Hodgdon for a powerful reading of Richard, the urinal scene and Clause 28; Hodgdon, 1998, 215–20).

The focus on Richard as ruthless tyrant, explored in Eyre and Loncraine, extends beyond fascist Europe as twenty-first century productions stage the play within a global context. Two prominent productions set *Richard III* in the Arab World: Sam Mendes's *Richard III*, staring Kevin Spacey, first performed at the Old Vic in 2011 and subsequently on tour around the globe; and Sulayman Al-Bassam's *Richard III: An Arab Tragedy*, staring Fayez Kazak, performed at the Swan Theatre in Stratford-Upon-Avon in 2007, then in Greece and Kuwait before traveling to the Kennedy Center in Washington, D.C., in 2009. Both productions feature prominently on the English stage—at the Old Vic and the RSC respectively; but both also move between the Gulf States and America as well, with the directors keenly aware of how their political allegory might resonate for contemporary global audiences.

These two productions provide a launching point for the next section's account of, and meditation on, adaptation more broadly. Ultimately I will ask us to raise questions about adapting Shakespeare for multinational audiences through the particular medium, made popular in the last two decades, of documentary film. This is because, in the case of both the Mendes and the Al-Bassam productions, the global reach of the stage play appears chronicled in documentary format, by Kevin Spacey, in *Now: In the Wings of the World Stage* (2014); and by Shakir Abal and Tim Langford for Al-Bassam's production in *Richard III: An Arab V.I.P.* (2011), both available for you to watch for yourself.

Libyan Richard

Sam Mendes and Kevin Spacey approach their production of *Richard III*, chronicled in a documentary film *Now: In the Wings of the World Stage* (2014), as a mode of instruction: "this 450-year-old play," they claim of *Richard III*, "can still teach us" (Mendes and Spacey, *Now* website). Specifically, it can teach us, as Spacey puts it, "about the nature of power." Mendes and Spacey call their collaboration the Bridge project: "The idea behind The Bridge Project," Mendes puts it, "was born out of a simple desire: a wish for artists, collaborators, and audiences on both sides of the Atlantic to experience one another's work, talent, and artistry in the theater" (Mendes and Spacey, *Now* website). The resulting production of *Richard III* spanned 200 performances and three continents, traveling from the Old Vic theater London to the deserts of Doha, across the Great Wall of China, through Istanbul, Singapore, Sydney, Naples, San Francisco, Beijing, and Hong Kong to New York City.

The accomplishment of the Bridge project is extraordinary, as the resulting documentary reveals. The film traces the *Richard III* production as it traverses the globe, toggling between scenes of the play in performance venues from Greece to China, and interviews with the actors who speak of the tremendous commitment and exhaustion attendant on such an ambitious project. But the ambition of the Bridge project, at least by Spacey and Mendes's own account, is more conscripted than global, limited to "both sides of the Atlantic." In this, the Bridge project is implicitly in dialogue with an earlier adaption of *Richard III*, offered in popularizing docudrama: Al Pacino's *Looking for Richard* (1996). This film tracked Pacino's NYC production of the play; and it, too, addressed Anglo-American audiences, specifically searching for an American mode of performing Shakespeare against what they deem the oppressive weight of the British Shakespeare legacy: "what's this thing," Pacino asks, "that gets between us [Americans] and Shakespeare?"

Attempting to translate Richard into modern parlance, Pacino drew his inspiration for Richard from American gangster culture, evoking his own performances in *Scarface* and *The Godfather* (see Salamon, 2000).

Such translation of Richard III, from British monarch to modern-day mafia don, has its dangers, as Adele Lee writes: "the Americanization of Shakespeare is, indeed, gradually resulting in 'dumbed-down' versions that have been 'rewritten in the idiom of mass culture'" (Lee, 2013, 160; Boose and Burt, 1997, 2). Equally cautionary, Stephen Greenblatt warns that the adaptation or rewriting of Shakespeare in modern terms might prove evocative but ultimately remain unsustained or unexplored, resulting in "the empty enumeration of meaningless parallels" or "the loss of specificity in a tangle of woolly generalities" (Greenblatt, 1998, 141). Neither Pacino, nor Spacey and Mendes, could be accused of offering a "dumbed-down" version of Shakespeare. Furthermore, the Mendes production featured nearly seventy percent of the original text and notably retained the female parts that have been so often cut in performance. Yet this production might indeed pose the challenge posited by Lee and Greenblatt, in that it offers a cultural parallel between Richard and contemporary politics that engages audiences while also, potentially, letting them off the hook.

Unlike Pacino's American mafia—which he interrogates as an Italian American—or Loncraine's portrait of European, including British, tyranny, Spacey offers a portrait of a tyrannical ruler from halfway around the world: specifically he draws on the iconography of Islamic fundamentalist rulers through Libya's Muammar Gaddafi. Spacey recounts, in an interview about the project, "we basically looked at a lot of photographs of [Muammar] Gaddafi and he is almost always wearing sunglasses . . . In fact, we based that entire costume on him—I even called it my 'Daf' look. [Laughs.]" (Cerasaro, 2014). For Spacey, this parallel of Richard with modern dictatorship offers a pedagogical opportunity: the play, he claims, teaches us about the nature of power in the modern era. Spacey says of Richard, "this is a man who is absolutely convinced that he has no conscience . . . he's cursed . . . Is there a way to make this man wake up to a conscience? . . . To allow that level, of 'he's actually a human being, despite the way he's behaved'?" ("Theater Talk, 'Kevin Spacey on Richard III,'" 2012). Richard III, in Spacey's view, is a trans-historical Vice figure, a Machiavel unbounded by history; he is a character who forces us to ask broad, universalizing questions, such as Spacey's: "what are the limits of the human?" But this charge of inhumanity against Gaddafi, when delivered to audiences in London and New York, might simply dehumanize Arab-world rulers already demonized by the West. What, in this case, is the play teaching us? This is not the same as Eyre's "it could have happened here," but rather, instead, look at what is happening over there. And this is an observation that might, as suggested above, let Western audiences off the hook, absent any interrogation of how the West might have participated in the rise of such tyranny.

Notice how different Spacey's view of Richard sounds from earlier renditions of the tyrant as pitiable or sympathetic under Garrick, Kean, and Aldridge. Spacey questions Richard's humanity altogether: can we call him human, "despite the way he's behaved"? To be fair, Mendes and Spacey imagine engaging their audiences in precisely this question. In their conception of the Bridge project, they seek answers by drawing on the theater houses to navigate the political landscape around them. Specifically, in referencing Gaddafi and the Arab Spring, Spacey and Mendes deploy modern media culture, and the representations of current events through news media, as a means of engaging the audience in the events onstage. Spacey recounts,

> as we were beginning the production, it just so happened that the Arab Spring erupted. And, Sam and I were both quite determined that the imagery that we were using throughout the play—the use of video and the kinds of ways in which we tried to make the play accessible and

modern and current and alive and in this moment —led us to making certain decisions like that, so that audiences were seeing our show and seeing images that they had already seen at some point on the news channels or they were going home after the performance was over and watching them on their news channels. So, it's sort of a testament to the fact that even this 450-year-old play can still teach us . . .

(Cerasaro, 2014).

Spacey's point—about the use of video as a way of making the production "accessible and modern and current and alive"— resonates with other recent versions of the play, so it is worth exploring in greater detail. But before turning to examine the use of digital media within productions of *Richard III*, we will first explore another appearance of Richard as Arab states allegory.

Gulf States Shakespeare

Kuwaiti director Sulayman Al-Bassam's *Richard III: An Arab Tragedy*, chronicled in Shakir Abal and Tim Langford's documentary film, *Richard III: An Arab V.I.P.* (2011), offers another version of Richard as political allegory. Emphasizing Shakespeare as a source of connection across cultures, Al-Bassam seeks to offer the "song" of Shakespeare in the Arab world through performance, even as he equally—and perhaps more forcefully—wants to bring the song of Arabic literature, as woven into the translation of Shakespeare through verse and music, to Britain and America. As Fayez Kazak puts it, "Whenever I sing you my song, and you sing me your song, then we become relatives on this earth. Otherwise we will be enemies" (Kazak, 2007). The work of bringing his song to Western audiences includes adapting the Shakespeare text to include well-known Arabic poetry, familiar to the play's Gulf States audiences if not its Western ones.

This vision of Al-Bassam, encapsulated in Fayez Kazak (who played Richard III), is more actively cross-cultural than the Bridge project, despite the global reach of both productions: the extensive tradition of Shakespeare performance in the Arab World, evoked by Al-Bassam, speaks back to, and informs, Western visions of Shakespeare (see Carlson and Litvin, 2016; Holderness, 2007 and 2013; Huang and Rivlin, 2014). Specifically *Richard III: An Arab Tragedy* deploys Shakespeare in two directions: to address issues within the Arab world, for Arab audiences; *and* to raise issues of Western interventionism with audiences in the West. It is worth unpacking these two ambitions at greater length to help address one of the final questions in this volume: in a book devoted to the language of Shakespeare, can a production change Shakespeare's language and remain true to the play?

Al-Bassam's first ambition is to use the medium of Shakespeare to raise questions in the Gulf States that might otherwise be censored. He notes of Kuwait that, even as it "has a specific level of freedom of expression that allows [a production like ours] to be made," nevertheless "it remains a conservative society, and there are de-facto rules. The three taboos are religion, politics, sex ... hence the utility of our friend William Shakespeare. It's William Shakespeare who is saying this, not us." The production, he claims, "allowed us to explore aspects of gulf life ... in ways that were quite liberating" (Brown, 2009). In his analysis of Al-Bassam's adaptations of Shakespeare (including *Richard II*, *Twelfth Night*, and *Hamlet* as well as *Richard III*), Graham Holderness—who has written extensively of his work—argues, "To some extent Shakespeare was a 'Trojan Horse' for Al-Bassam, a cultural monument that enabled him to smuggle critical views on his own society past the authorities and to the greedy intelligences of the theatre audience" (Holderness, 2007, 128). For the actors, as well as the audiences, the parallels between Richard III and contemporary leadership were obvious: "Richard is still here in every Arab country," claims Nadine Joma'a (Lady Anne). Nicholas Daniel (Hastings) elaborates: "if you take Shakespeare's plays and look at them through the times we are living in the Arab world, you'll find Shakespeare is practically writing about *us*" (Lee, 2013, 161). Staging Shakespeare offers a mechanism for discussing current events: if Shakespeare's play is educational, its value lies in teaching Arab audiences about themselves, "about *us*."

Al-Bassam elaborates on this process of adapting Shakespeare for Arab audiences when he says that he strives to "put contemporary figures in the political landscape within the fabric of another world, a Shakespearean world, and thereby open up a space for dissent, or a space for another kind of annotation" (Al-Bassam, 2006). It is this interest in "dissent," or "annotation," that motivates his production: he hopes to provoke conversations after the performance itself. The act of interpretation and deciphering leads to discursive space or, indeed, a new kind of theater—emerging out of the dissent, analysis, and insight of the audience—after the official theater curtain has gone down. Al-Bassam continues, saying "Current political events—and our perceptions of them—hang like a misty landscape, half-perceived, in the backdrop of the play" (Holderness, 2013). The protection of allegory—the "misty landscape, half-perceived"—allows the director and actors (in a move resonant with a long history of dissident productions of Shakespeare) to interrogate contemporary tyrannies while remaining at a cultural and temporal distance. For example, as the World Shakespeare Congress in Prague (2010) highlighted, a long tradition of translating and performing Shakespeare in the Czech Republic upholds dissident performances during times of censorship, under Nazi and Soviet occupations, for example. Such resistant conversation might even reach the corridors of power: the President of Syria, to Al-Bassam's surprise, appeared as a member of the audience one evening.

The second ambition of *Richard III: Arab Tragedy* is to offer commentary on the role of American or of Western states generally in the Middle East. "Showing this play in the United States has a special meaning," Fayez Kazak says, "because it is addressing so many concerns that have arisen in the recent catastrophic period in the whole region, because America played a significant role in it. We are going to meet the audience above all" (*Richard III: An Arab V.I.P.*, 2010). This idea of "meet[ing] the [Western] audience above all" is a driving force behind the production. Performing *Richard III: An Arab Tragedy* first at the Royal Shakespeare Company in Stratford-Upon-Avon (the first Arabic language production ever commissioned there), and then in Washington, D.C., at the Kennedy Center, this production truly attempted to speak truth to power. "The objective of art," as Al-Bassam succinctly puts it, "is to ask difficult questions" (*Richard III: An Arab V.I.P.*, 2010). Keenly aware of the representation of Islamic states in the Western media, the actors and director hoped to speak back to those nations that have been so present, violently and disruptively, in their homelands: "We are part of the axis of evil . . . we are bored of this topic, it sounds like a devil's song," says Amal Omran (Margaret) in *An Arab V.I.P.* Al-Bassam echoes this sentiment: "There are so many prejudices and so many ready made formulas to identify that Arab World, and to identify that Gulf World, that are negative, that are negative prejudices" (Brown, 2009). In its performance at Washington, D.C.'s Kennedy Center, Al-Bassam hoped for President Obama's attendance. He sought to draw attention to "the whole history of Western intervention and mismanagement and violence in the region."

In offering what we might call a double adaptation—namely, presenting Arab audiences with a Shakespeare character right out of their contemporary political moment, *and* presenting Western audiences with an Arab tragedy drawn from Shakespeare—Al-Bassam departs from the goals of Mendes and Spacey. While *Now*'s production of *Richard III* remains true to Shakespeare's script, bringing the bard around the globe, Al-Bassam translates Shakespeare in several ways in order to adapt the playwright for multiple modern audiences. First, he literally translates the playtext into Arabic. He then rewrites some of the imagery to resonate in a Gulf World, and Islamic, idiom. Finally, he weaves Shakespeare's script with poetic language from classical Arabic, including the Qur'an, as well as from modern Arabic poetry. The result is, Holderness writes, "a 'cross-cultural' poetic sensibility capable of interweaving all these strands and producing from them a new theatrical discourse" (Holderness, 2007, 131). *Richard III: An Arab Tragedy* ultimately puts pressure on Shakespeare as the bard of Stratford. For, as Holderness asks, "if the Shakespeare dispersed by linguistic imperialism around the globe is also a Shakespeare wholly or partially 'hybridised' by contact with other languages and cultures, then is it still the same old imperial Shakespeare?" (Holderness and Loughrey, 2006, 30). Or is it possible, as Dennis Kennedy puts it, that "almost from the start of his importance as the idealized English dramatist there have been other Shakespeares, Shakespeares not dependent on English and often at odds with it?" (Kennedy, 1993, 2).

This is a version of the question we posed above: what happens to Shakespeare when his language is modified and adapted for new uses? Is this form of adaptation radically distinct from the other adaptations we've studied in this chapter, such as amplifying Richard's sympathetic potential, or using Shakespeare's script to present Richard as Hitler or Gaddafi? On one level, yes, to modify Shakespeare's language is to change his legacy: he comes to us as words on the page, and this volume is devoted to helping you understand those words precisely because they are at the heart of Shakespeare's play in all its complexity. But on another level, one might take up Al-Bassam's argument as an invitation: Shakespeare from the start invited adaptation and transmutation because, particularly in a play like *Richard III*, this is at the center of his own enterprise. Shakespeare takes a story, modifies it, exaggerates and even sensationalizes it. Modern directors thus follow Shakespeare's own lead in transposing the play to their own times.

Al-Bassam hopes that his own version of a non-English Shakespeare—a Shakespeare beyond English nation and language, in a hybrid form with global reach—will teach audiences in the Arab world, Britain, and America simultaneously. If Spacey and Mendes, too, emphasize the educational outcome of the play, Al-Bassam specifically adapts—alters, shifts, revises—Shakespeare in order to educate audiences about contemporary cultural particularities and interconnections. He wants to challenge audiences to move beyond their own positionality to see themselves through the eyes of another. If Arab-world actors and audiences appear, by the accounts above, to embrace the production's opportunity, American audiences—at least from Al-Bassam's vantage point—did not. The Kennedy Center production failed to generate the kinds of conversations he had hoped. Even as the play ends with Richmond as a "platitude-spouting Christian US general who at the play's conclusion announces the instillation of an interim government," American audiences saw their own notions of Arab tyranny and fundamentalism confirmed rather than challenged (Holderness, 2013; Marlowe, 2007). As a result, as Adele Lee points out in her analysis of the film version, "so disheartened has Al-Bassam become that in a recent interview in *Rolling Stone* magazine he revealed that he's decided to no longer produce political plays, since 'he has devoted so much of himself to his work without seeing it foster any kind of political change'" (Lee, 2013, 169). Having hoped that President Obama might attend the production, Al-Bassam and his actors are left to hope for change without necessarily seeing any: "Because of the policies of the U.S. I have always objected to going to this country," says Carole Abboud (Elizabeth) in *An Arab V.I.P.* But, she continues, "the American people have proven something when they elected Obama. But what did they prove? This is what we have to wait and see."

Studying these two theatrical productions side by side, this portion of the chapter has sought to tease out the quite similar, but culturally distinct, ambitions of each in order to pose questions about adaptation more broadly. At times, as the above discussion suggests of the process of adaptation, Shakespeare is invoked as a static sage, informing modern audiences of insights offered 450 years ago; at other points

Shakespeare seems to be a cypher, allowing current conversations to occur in spaces that might otherwise forbid or ignore them. The West, Al-Bassam's project seems to posit, is deaf to the conditions of the Arab world; but filtered through Shakespeare, Arab theater at least earns a seat at the RSC and the Kennedy Center.

Digital Richard

This chapter proposes to end its discussion of *Richard III* by turning to the question of form, asking why, in the last two decades, such prominent productions of the play have both deployed digital media in their performances (think of Spacey's "news channels"), and used film to chronicle the stage production in documentary form.

To take the issue of digital media in productions first, we might say, with Spacey, that the video of news channel images in the theater itself, combined with the audience's own memory of televised events of the Arab Spring, help the play's allegory to come to life. Mendes relies on digital technologies to make his play contemporary. Richard Loncraine, too, draws heavily on media technologies in his *Richard III*. Richard persistently replays the silent film documenting his own coronation, for example, as if to suggest that the real practice of kingship fails in comparison to the video recording of it. The film also deploys "35mm still photography, photograph-based silk-screen graphic art, wireless telegraphy and tickertape, recorded and amplified 'live' sound, and, in the final moments, digital collage" (Donaldson, 2002, 244). It is a veritable catalogue of media forms, incorporated to amplify the play's effect on its audiences.

To begin our exploration of media and *Richard III* let me ask you a question: how might digital technologies, deployed within stage and film versions of *Richard III*, amplify or distract from your own understanding of this volume's primary focus, the play's language? What effect does it have, to see ticker tape or video projections or surveillance technology surrounding you in the theater, or on screen? Here I invite you to think for yourself, as an interpreter not only of the play but of modern culture. And I even invite you to explore this question through writing (see below). In the meantime I'll offer just one answer. It's an answer that might surprise you, since you might (reasonably) expect a Shakespeare critic such as myself to find modern technologies distracting.

I'd argue that these media forms help draw out a tension within the play's language itself. Certainly, both Loncraine and Mendes/Spacey find that media technology helps to disseminate information in their productions: media is how the audience understands this story as a modern political allegory, having already seen such events on our screens in the form of Hitler's rallies, the fall of the Berlin Wall, or the events of the Arab Spring. But these references to media technologies arguably have another effect, too. That is, they amplify our passivity as the viewing audience—we are watching someone watching a television. This position, of audience passivity, is one that Shakespeare explores in his own playtext. How do we respond to Richard's questions, for example, throughout the play? Or his asides to us? We are his silent partners, watching but unable to affect events onstage. Modern productions that use media technologies exaggerate this effect, casting us as the viewers who inhabit a sofa or chair, inert as violence erupts around us.

Shakespeare's Richard is a highly theatrical character. He deploys theater constantly, to woo Anne, to justify the execution of Hastings, and to feign reluctance in assuming the crown. He uses props, like Bishops and books; he stage manages actors, like Buckingham; he studies lines. He even models himself on theatrical characters directly, like the Vice or Machiavel. The theatrical effects can reinforce our own position as unwitting but conscripted participants: we know that he's donning a costume but we can't warn the characters onstage. We can do little to influence events, and instead watch them unfold knowingly. The introduction of modern media in Loncraine and Mendes draws explicit attention to this gap, between actions unfolding in front of us, and our own passive response of them. Those in power have access to narrative forms, capturing events through theater, television, video, or film. The powerless watch and comment, from the citizens to the Scrivener to ourselves. Donaldson puts it starkly in arguing that Loncraine's *Richard III* "uses allusions to and techniques characteristic of silent cinema as emblems of death, framing the story of Richard as an allegory of the role of cinema and other modern media in the institution and maintenance of death-dealing social regimes . . . Loncraine uses this wide range of reframed communications technologies in order to characterize Richard as a modern, media-reliant dictator" (Donaldson, 2002, 244).

If a dictator might rely on media for his rise—be it the theater, in the case of Shakespeare's Richard, or video feed in the case of Mendes's and Loncraine's Richard as Nazi allegory—modern audiences also recognize how video and film will preserve this political trauma in perpetuity. Screened footage reminds us that those events occurring right before us, in the present tense, will soon turn into the past: future audiences might view the surveillance footage of our night at the theater; or they might view the events onstage in the form of video feed. Events are in real time, and belated, all at once. And this is precisely what Shakespeare illuminates in the play, from the time of its first productions: Richard is a character from history books, brought to life through a new media, namely the early modern theater. What's uncomfortable for Shakespeare's own audiences—where do they stand in relation to this history?—remains uncomfortable for modern viewers, too. How do we appear, in the video and newsfeed of Richard's rise? Collaborators? Silent witnesses? Or members of a resistance, whatever that might look like? These questions about positionality—asking, where do we stand?—might explain, to turn to our second issue of media invoked at the start of this section, the popularity of the documentary form. It is a form that secures intention, and allows second chances, as we will see.

Documentary Richard

Mendes and Al-Bassam, as well as Pacino, offer hybrid projects that feature both a staged production *and* a filmed version. The form has an obvious commercial appeal: directors and producers reach a much greater audience through film, as the success of the NT Live program has proven. Further, documentary brings the issues of *Richard III* into, as Spacey's title indicates, the *now*. The play becomes not an introduction to British history, reliant on knowledge of the Wars of the Roses and the rise of the Tudor dynasty. Instead, the play offers an intelligent and timely commentary on the spread of tyrannical power in the contemporary world around us. Theater and film productions do this as well, of course, as Loncraine's *Richard III* attests. But in mounting a documentary, the filmmakers are able to communicate directly their own hopes for the production and how an audience might receive it. The documentary film genre is, Lee writes, "more didactic in nature as the primary purpose of a documentary is usually to present the audience with an argument and reinforce a certain ideological position ... the documentary form privileges the political and ethical stance of the filmmaker, providing him/her with the means to make audiences conscious of a problem and to win their support" (Lee, 2013, 170). Another interesting effect of documentary lies in the blurring of fiction and reality: rather than insisting upon the distinction between staging the play, and the play itself, the documentary form obscures the boundary between play and world: "Like Al Pacino's *Looking for Richard*, *Richard III: An Arab V.I.P.* makes it difficult to determine when actors are in or out of character, and which parts constitute the 'drama' and which the 'documentary'" (Lee, 2013, 171).

To take the example of Al Pacino's *Richard III*, performed in the theater and chronicled in a documentary, *Looking for Richard*: arguably, Pacino assumes the role of Richard not as theater, but as biography. Emily Bartels writes how the documentary "provides a richly passionate example of the play's and Shakespeare's immediacy—not only as it frames the play, but, more potently, as its frames breakdown. As Shakespeare's scenes dominate more and more of the focus, Pacino seems to *become* Richard (at least the Richard we get before his fall), his role as mediator itself mediated by the play" (Bartels, 1997, 59). Indeed, it's not just that Pacino comes to inhabit Richard. It's that he seems, one might argue, to have been Richard all along. From his appearance in *Scarface* (1983), Pacino adopts a Richard III-style role. In this a gangster film inspired by the Richard III plot, the hero Tony Montana is, like Richard, physically deformed and cursed by his mother, acting out with ruthless, murderous ambition. Pacino's triumph in *Scarface* led to other gangster roles, including his role as Michael Corleone in *The Godfather*. Pacino's death at the end of his production of *Richard III* in fact replicates this earlier film, a point that Hodgdon makes in her analysis of the play and its adaptations: he "repeats his own demise as Michael Corleone in Coppola's *Godfather, Part 3* (1990), as well as that of Jimmy Cagney's Eddie Bartlett in *The Roaring Twenties* (1939), repositioning Richard III, *Richard III*, and *Looking for Richard* within a long cinematic tradition of gangster films and memorable heroes" (Hodgdon, 1998, 214). Performance thus becomes a kind of doubling and redoubling, what might be called with Barbara Hodgdon, after W.B. Worthen and Joseph Roach, "a collaborative body project, one that brings together Shakespeare's body (as his text) with those of the actor, the character, and the spectator" (Hodgdon, 1998, 208).

If contemporary Richards speak to audiences with immediacy, his effect on us can produce mixed results. Al-Bassam's experience staging *Richard III: An Arab Tragedy* at the Kennedy Center in Washington, D.C., illuminates the challenge of this project of adaptation for the theater: making audiences "conscious of a problem" in the space of one night, as Al-Bassam aims to do, is no easy task. Dominant ideologies and cultural narratives can work to frustrate such recognition.

Theater does, of course, have the singular power of live-ness. The experience of watching a play, particularly in a crowded, energized space, makes possible the kind of dramatic audience responses chronicled from Aristotle forward. Yet for twenty-first-century audiences steeped in screen life, documentary film offers a chance at familiar, extended, repetitive engagement. Herein lies its appeal. It offers, one might argue, the director and actors a second chance: what might have failed, in the theater itself, to provoke the "dissent" and "annotation" that Al-Bassam seeks instead can be watched again and again on a television, computer, or phone. Witnessing footage from Damascus, Beirut, Baghdad, Abu Dhabi, Kuwait City, London, and Washington, D.C., an audience of *Richard III: An Arab V.I.P.* might just realize what Al-Bassam's *Richard III: An Arab Tragedy* hoped for but did not see: political change through song.

Revisions and transpositions

Finally, it is worth exploring, in the tradition of Cibber, even more radical forms of adapting Shakespeare's *Richard III*. We've already encountered one such adaptation, or inspiration, from Shakespeare: Josephine Tey's *The Daughter of Time* (1951). This mystery novel offers an entirely different, and often entertaining, mode of adaption: a detective story about the guilt of Richard III, investigated by a detective confined to his bed by an injury. So, too, with Pacino's *Godfather*, which presents a modern transposition of the role in the mafia don Michael Corleone. We can end this chapter by briefly invoking a third: Kevin Spacey's Frank Underwood in *House of Cards*. This role casts Spacey as a Washington, D.C., politician, manipulating himself into greater and greater positions of power. For one critic and viewer, Elsie Walker, the parallels between Richard and Underwood are haunting: "I cannot watch House of Cards," she writes, "without feeling haunted by his predecessor. Keeping the play in mind, superimposing it upon a viewing of House of Cards like a thin layer of tracing paper, makes both the darker and playful details of the show more perceivable. Equally, for all Richmond's closing platitudes at the end of Shakespeare's play, it is as if Richard has found a new way to life. He has escaped the grave and moved from England. Frank is the new "boar" who devours ribs, hates children, wields the power of his Lady Macbeth-like wife, and needs no horse" (Walker, 2014, 411).

Walker's invocation of Richard escaping the grave can be our final note in this chapter on adapting Richard: through adaptation, has Richard indeed "escaped the grave and moved from England"? Has he moved across Europe, to the Gulf States, through China and Singapore to Washington, D.C., and then back to England? Certainly, given precisely the reach of the two global productions of *Richard III* studied in this chapter, yes. Further, from an historical rather than geographical vantage point, one might argue that the preoccupation with this king, perpetuated over centuries in large part by the success of Shakespeare's play, helped to fuel the search for, and discovery of, the real king's body: what might have remained adaptation, a body coming alive onstage and in film in the form of an actor, has led back eerily to Richard's physical bones themselves, his skeleton—which has indeed escaped its anonymous grave to be reinterred at Leicester Cathedral.

To see this process of Richard's resurrection and internment chronicled, I invite you to view programs such as the Channel 4 documentary *Richard III: The King in the Car Park* (2013) and the PBS *Secrets of the Dead: Resurrecting Richard* (2016). Here you can watch historians and scientists test DNA remains of the skeleton unearthed in a Leicester car park. The discovery of Richard's body, and the reconstruction of his spinal remains in particular, have served to excite further debates, debates that have flourished before, through, and beyond Shakespeare's rendition of Richard's life. As Philip Schwyzer's book on the remains of Richard III notes, "the play, in spite of its own pessimistic assumptions about history, has become the medium whereby certain fragments and remains of a long-lost world

live on into the present day" (Schwyzer, 2013). Now I invite
you to pick up your pen (or open your computer) and join the
discussion.

Writing matters

Adaptation and editing

As Catherine Belsey reminds us in her volume on *Romeo and
Juliet* for this series, there is no better way to come to grips
with adaptation than to do one yourself. So for this prompt, I
invite you to pick a scene and adapt it however you like. You
might adapt it as a different genre: a comedy, a western, a
horror film or a graphic novel. Or you might radically adapt
the play: translate the script into another language, or produce
a silent film version of it (as some of my students did).
Suggestions for your adaptation: the difficult scene of
prophecies; or the famous opening lines; or the battle of
Bosworth.

Alternately, in line with Jane Smiley's *A Thousand Acres*,
which rewrites *King Lear* from the point of view of Goneril
and Regan, imagine rewriting the story of Richard III from a
new perspective. You might tell the story of the king from the
point of view of Clarence, the nephews, or Margaret; you
might imagine retelling the story as one about disability and
prejudice. Finally, you might want to retell the story of Richard
based on the new evidence about his remains. The point of this
thought-experiment is to expose the creativity and ingenuity
behind the process of adaptation; and to illuminate the crucial
role of Shakespeare's language in keeping Richard's story alive.

If adapting a Shakespeare play is one way of firmly analyzing
the text and seeing what makes it tick, another is to edit it. As
any editor will tell you, there is no greater intimacy with a text
than editing, because one must pay attention to linguistic
details beyond one's own interests. In an assignment indebted
to Frances Dolan's volume in this series, consider editing a

particular scene or speech. Look up the speech in the first quarto edition of 1597, available online through a resource like Internet Shakespeare Editions (http://internetshakespeare. uvic.ca/Library/Texts/R3/). Then find the same speech or scene online in an edition like the MIT Shakespeare, which offers you the full text but without an editorial apparatus (in contrast to your Arden Shakespeare, which gives you extremely full notes). Imagine how you might edit your chosen speech or scene: what words need explanation? What sentences? Are there dense images, twisted syntactical structures, highly visible rhetorical flourishes? Begin by circling those words, phrases and exchanges that interest you and write about why. From there, you can then turn to lexicographical research, looking up the various meanings of key words to help you in deciphering the passage(s). As you complete your editing, turn to write about the passage itself, with a particular eye to what surprised you and what you learned through this editing process.

CHAPTER FOUR

Writing Tips and Topics

From his page to yours: Turning reading into writing

My first piece of advice as you begin writing is so familiar that you might just sigh: read the play again. Read and re-read. Take notes—in the margin, on a piece of paper, in an open Word file on your computer. I also think it is worth watching at least two productions of the play, so that you are able to see the words on stage, in action. You might consider Benedict Cumberbatch's *Richard III*, as part of the *Hollow Crown* series; and the versions by Olivier and McKellen. Follow along with your texts, noticing additions and cuts. These directorial choices might help spur your thinking, particularly if you find yourself disagreeing with choices. Take notes on your responses and build up from there.

Most of the chapters in this book have helped hone what might be called your detective skills: I've asked you, throughout, to study your evidence carefully. That is, I've asked you to consider the play's language, for this is your primary evidence—we've worked to understand how this language arrived on the page, what it means, and how it is constructed. Good arguments, like good detection, will emerge from careful consideration of your primary evidence. But good writing, to continue the analogy, is also motivated by questions: who did it, why, and can we prove it? I often think of writing a paper as a form of answering a good question (a better question than my "who-dunnit" one here), and answering it through a clear story. Let's examine this process. But first, let's examine the nature of your assignment itself, whether it is pre-assigned or self-generated. I have tips for both situations.

Your topic

Often you'll be given a question or set of questions from your professor, teacher, or examiner. What might seem straightforward—answer the prompt—is actually more complicated, because sometimes the best answers (or at least the most sophisticated ones) come from interrogating the question or prompt itself, or figuring out a way to shape it so that you can provide as rich an answer as possible. For example, in one of the prompts in Chapter Two, I suggested that you analyze the animal imagery in the play. This is a tall order, because the play is filled with animal imagery. A paper that seeks to answer the prompt by surveying all the animals will probably fail to offer as strong an argument as possible because it will inevitably fall into description instead. So it is useful to interrogate the question: what animals? Invoked by whom? Thus you might narrow the question by asking, who uses this imagery and why? When Margaret describes Richard as a bunch-backed toad, why does she use that particular image? Or you might ask, what types of animals does she invoke—meat-eating mammals, or cold-blooded reptiles? If it's both, you might choose to concentrate on one or the other; or you might choose to analyze why she ranges so freely through the animal world. Rather than focusing on imagery deployed by one character, you might instead concentrate closely on one or two examples, narrowing the question so that your answer can have more depth. You might consider the boar. Finally, think about the implications of the prompt or your argument: does the use of this imagery cause us to come to Richard's defense (or defense of the animals), or do we feel he is dehumanized, and therefore easier to hate?

I'm offering advice here on navigating a survey-style question. But your writing prompt might instead ask you a large question that appears to elicit a yes or no answer: Does Richard hate women? Is the play propaganda? Is Richard evil? In each of these cases, you might answer yes, or no. You might also—as suggested above—interrogate the question. What women? Does he seem to mock all women, or just particular ones—if so, why? What is propaganda? Here you might turn to the play itself to see how characters deploy what we could call propaganda (using false information for political purposes). Or you could consider how propaganda is written for particular purposes at specific moments in time. Does the play continue to work as propaganda five hundred years after the historical events, or does the temporal vantage point shift our experience of the play? Finally, you might ask, what is evil? How was the term defined in Shakespeare's day? Is evil based in action or intention? Is it framed in secular or religious terms?

Here I'm encouraging you to interrogate the terms of the prompt itself so that you are on clear ground before starting, and so that you begin to shape your response into an argument. Furthermore, in each of these cases you might want to limit yourself to one or two scenes or exchanges so that you have a manageable amount of material. But most importantly, after defining your terms and limiting the range of your answer to an amount of text reasonable to the size of the paper, then you'll want to think about whether you want to answer yes or no—or whether your answer is more like "yes, but," or "yes and no." Yes, you might argue, Richard does seem to hate women, in that he manipulates and discards them (Anne), mocks them (Margaret and Elizabeth), and ignores them. At the same time, you might also argue that he seems to hate many characters, both male and female, and he certainly manipulates them all. So then the answer might consider, in what ways is his attitude toward women singular? How does he treat women differently? Or you might want to ask, why does he condemn women? He might appear to tell us: it's because he cannot prove a lover. But is it a good idea to take Richard at his word?

Besides which, his is not a full answer, since he proceeds to woo and marry Anne in the next scene. What I'm suggesting here is that apparent yes or no questions are an opportunity to take one side or another, if you feel strongly; but perhaps more interestingly, they offer a chance to step back and explore how something might be both affirmative and negative at once. This is the complexity of literature, and Shakespeare.

If you need to devise your own topic, I'll offer you some advice that I use myself when I write: most frequently, I start at the sentence level. What word, or sentence, or exchange, sparks my curiosity? What sticks with me, and keeps my attention? What frustrates my understanding? Often I'll find that it is a word or phrase that is improbably beautiful in the circumstances, or a phrase I can't quite figure out. My PhD thesis emerged from a single phrase: "the pale cast of thought," used by Hamlet. My thesis did not study *Hamlet*—but this image of a "pale cast" for thought captivated me and I began my investigations into materialized speech there. So trust your own instincts and hunches—often the words or sentences or exchanges that stick with you are trying to tell you something, so follow them. If nothing has sparked you yet, re-read the play, keeping the above questions in mind.

I do have students and colleagues who work in the opposite direction. They are interested in particular issues or questions, and these questions propel their writing. In this case, you might have a general sense of a topic: you might know you are interested in law in Shakespeare; or the representation of race or gender; or the relationship of fools to truth. Here the challenge becomes, in the space of a single paper, how do you limit your investigation to a scene or character or speech, particularly with an eye to surprising yourself at the results of what you find? For, often the best arguments come out of the unexpected. To take an example from a recent class: a student who is compelled by notions of evil, studying evil and ambition through Nietzsche's theory of the Übermensch (super man) or Machiavelli's *The Prince*, might find Richard a compelling study. But how to limit it? Here, one might decide to limit it by studying Richard in comparison to a passage in Nietzsche or Machiavelli, seeing how one of his speeches confirms or challenges (or both) these political theorists. Or one might limit the topic instead by comparing Richard's own sense of his villainy with the views of other characters. Is there one notion of what constitutes a villain in the play? Or many? Asking such questions, my student began to concentrate on the link of wit to evil in the play, exploring why only Richard seemed to have access to wit, and how this skill might presage or expose his villainy.

So if you know, going in, that you want to examine a particular topic or issue (because it is the topic that appears in most of your writing regardless of the text) then I'm suggesting how you might interrogate or deepen your own interests: narrow the scope of your investigation, or closely define your terms in a new historical and literary context (Shakespeare's sixteenth century). My most pressing piece of advice here: be curious. Rather than knowing your answers ahead of time, let your investigations surprise you.

Tips on writing

Focus

Regardless of whether your topic is assigned or self-generated, you will need to find a focus, as I began to suggest above. Your focus is not the same as your argument: the focus is how you decide to limit your investigations. Boundaries of some kind are almost always generative: good fences, we might say in a twist on Robert Frost, make good papers. One of the simplest and often most-effective ways of focusing a paper is to pick a very limited amount of text to concentrate on: one scene, minor portions of two scenes, a speech. It is not a weakness to choose such a limited focus, since it will allow you to analyze your portion of the play in more depth. A broad focus over the whole play will consign you to generalized summary without much insightful analysis. Furthermore, in focusing on one or two scenes or speeches, you should still consider your chosen bit of text in relation to the rest of the play: how does the scene connect thematically and symbolically with other scenes? How does the scene recall earlier moments in the play, and to what ends? Are the images in your key speech repeated elsewhere with changed meanings?

Evidence

Shakespeare's language is your best, most sophisticated evidence, so use it wisely. This language is rarely straightforward, as we've seen throughout this book. If I were to paraphrase Richard's opening lines, "Now is the winter of our discontent / Made glorious summer by this son of York" (1.1.1–2), in the style of SparkNotes by saying, "The war is over and the York family won," I would only be catching a fraction of the meaning of the line. Richard's pun on sun/son, his use of natural images whereby autumn and winter will inevitably follow summer (thereby subtly suggesting the potential fall of Edward), his use of the communal "our" despite his own sense of alienation from the family—these are all details contained in the language of those two lines. Analyzing portions of the text in such detail will allow you to prove, and deepen, your argument. Because Shakespeare's language is rich and dense, I would advise you to quote only four to six lines at a time, rather than large chunks of text. That is, unless you have chosen, or are assigned, a longer speech to analyze in full—in which case, I'd still recommend breaking the speech into shorter sections to help structure your analysis. Attempting to analyze a long section all at once can lead to summary and generalization. Use shorter phrases and lines, giving yourself space to analyze them fully.

Developing an argument

Remember that the play is an art form that has been constructed. In analyzing the scene or speech, pay attention to why the scene/speech is constructed as it is, and what effect it has on the meaning of the play: does it contribute to or complicate the themes, images, or implications of the play? Do not focus on how the characters feel, as if they were real people, but instead focus on how they are represented by Shakespeare; you might ask, why does he construct characters' feelings in a particular way, for example? You should write a unified essay and not a series of summaries of events and/or character's traits. Find a central argument and thesis that helps to illuminate your topic—do not fall into the trap of supplying irrelevant plot summary and description. Cite the text in order to bolster your claims and to focus the reader's attention on specific aspects of language central to your thesis, but do not waste your time in paraphrasing the text.

This advice helps you to hone and deepen your argument. But how do you find an argument in the first place? The prospect of finding an original argument on a Shakespeare play can be daunting. But as my mentor and colleague Susanne Wofford said to me, in sound advice I'll pass on to you, no one has ever analyzed a Shakespeare play from your vantage point. You are in a new generation, analyzing Shakespeare in a time and place that has never existed before. You've been trained differently than critics before you, both formally in the classroom, and informally through life experiences. This doesn't mean that your argument should be about *you*. It simply means that you have the potential to see the Shakespeare play differently than those who have come before you; and you have the ability to express your observations in new ways. Even if you are analyzing something deeply familiar to generations of critics—the opening speech of the play, for example—there is still an opportunity for you to be surprising in your argument and conclusions.

To me, the best arguments ultimately emerge out of a question that is compelling to the paper's author. Even if it is a question that has been asked many times—is *Richard III* a piece of propaganda?—if it is the question that pulls at you, go for it. Find your angle. Figure out a way to make your answer

168   KING RICHARD III: LANGUAGE AND WRITING

fresh. Approach the question from an unexpected vantage point. That's my own advice. Forge ahead with what draws you, and find your way to make it new. One way of doing this: ask a question about your topic (whether it's a speech, scene or character that's compelled you, or it's an issue that's tugging at you) that you can't answer easily. Then set about figuring out how to answer it, using the play's language as evidence in constructing your answer. You might need to reframe the question as you go. If you begin to realize that your question is too general, you might need to focus it. Rather than asking whether *Richard III* is propaganda, you might narrow it: does *Richard III* function as a complement to the Tudor Queen Elizabeth? Or, does Shakespeare follow Thomas More's condemnation of Richard, or does his play vary in its sympathies?

I'm suggesting that you follow your own interests and build a paper from there—if you're at liberty to design your own topic. I should warn you, though: some Shakespeareans would argue differently, and I feel obliged to tell you their advice, too. Some might counsel you to start by finding something new—a new angle, an unposed question. If generations of critics have discussed gender in *Twelfth Night*, they might say, that topic has been done; and you need to select another topic that's more cutting edge. In the case of *Richard III*, a number of critics in disability studies have studied the play, so one might argue that analyzing Richard in terms of early modern disability has been exhausted. My own advice: forge ahead anyway. Ask the question that interests you, even if it is familiar. Just find a way of answering that feels fresh, an angle that's been under-explored. And you can assess the freshness of your own argument by turning, after you've gone as far as possible by yourself, to your edition's introduction, to your lecture notes, and to a select number of secondary articles on your topic (the articles listed in this volume's bibliography will be of help to you). If you find that your paper is stating an argument that has been clearly established by others, try to reframe your question so that you are offering something new:

expand existing arguments by considering a scene or character that's been overlooked; or modify those arguments by moving in a slightly different direction. In a nutshell, I'm suggesting you build up from your own interests, and then revise toward as fresh and compelling an approach as possible.

Organization

A good paper, like most good stories, has a beginning, a middle, and an end. If organization is a sticking point for you, try telling the story of your argument aloud to yourself or a friend, in simple terms. You might find that you begin with the question that started you thinking, such as "is *Richard III* a form of propaganda?" And then you might offer your answer, "Even as it might replicate some of the propagandistic attacks on Richard, the play provokes a complex and often sympathetic response to this villain." From there, what would you expect next? I'd expect an example. "For example, in his opening soliloquy, Richard offers some justifications for his exceptional, and villainous, status." From here, you might analyze the references in his speech to his own deformity and isolation. Notice how you have moved from the general to the specific, from your opening question to an answer (your argument) to an analysis of a piece of evidence supporting your answer (proof). From here, you might pan out again, to a second example of how the play moves beyond propaganda. "Shakespeare also shapes a villain who is both funny and intimate with the audience, in contrast to the play's other characters." Here is another form of proof: Richard isn't just exceptional in being "deformed," he is also exceptional in his humor and intimacy with us. Here, again, you'll pick a scene or speech to analyze. I might turn to the lines about Clarence, or the soliloquy after Anne's departure.

I hope you're getting the idea here: move through your paper logically, as if you are telling a story and unfolding it clearly to a listening audience. This method, deceptively simple, demands that you employ a narrative structure in shaping your argument, rather than offering a series of bullet points, or a superimposed structure based in abstract categories. A bullet-point structure might move from one character to another: "The play's contribution to propaganda appears in its portraits of Richard, Margaret, the princes, and Richmond." While such a form of organization might work (especially if you were exploring how some characters are more incendiary as propaganda than others) notice that this method of organization is not based on your argument but upon a list. You are just moving from one character to another, rather than driving forward a larger argument. As a result, papers based on bullet points or lists can grow repetitious.

The other pitfall, using a superimposed structure, can have the opposite problem: it can be hard to follow. If, for example, you looked up a definition of propaganda as "information, especially of a biased or misleading nature, used to promote a political cause or point of view" you might be tempted to organize your paper according to the principles invoked in the definition. You might have a paragraph on how Shakespeare gives us biased information, seen in Richard's view of himself as a villain (i.e. no one sees him as a good man). Then you could have a paragraph on how the play misleads us (implying Richard's murder of the princes, which isn't proven). Then, in a classic five-paragraph essay with three body paragraphs, you'd have a final body paragraph on how the play promotes a particular political cause (Richmond wins and the Tudors triumph). Perhaps such a paper could be successful—but the danger is that you are importing a "foreign" structure on the play. Does your reader care if you prove the Wikipedia-style definition of propaganda to be true for this play? Are these three terms—biased and misleading information, and political principles—crucial to the play itself? Such arguments can be hard to follow because they aren't following a logic organic to the play.

Often the clearer mode of organization is based around Shakespeare's play itself. For example, instead of using a

Wikipedia-style definition of propaganda, consider analyzing scenes about misleading information. This way you could shift from an external, and not especially illuminating, framework on propaganda to investigate instead how Shakespeare meditates on the nature of distorted information in the play itself. Here you might move from one problematic document to another: the warrant for Clarence's death, supplied by Richard, not King Edward; the Scrivener's indictment against Hastings; and Buckingham and Richard's allegations of Edward's "contract with Lady Lucy," proving the illegitimacy of the princes. Richard deploys biased or misleading information throughout the play, and meditating on these moments will help refine your thinking on the question of propaganda more broadly.

Alternately, on the topic of *Richard III* as propaganda, you might turn to definitions of the term in political theory, starting with the *OED*. If you were to do so, you'd find that the word "propaganda" is not in common use in English until the nineteenth century. The term appears in 1679 in relation to the Catholic Church's Congregation of Propaganda, but its modern designation as biased or misleading information appears in use around 1820. You might nonetheless decide that Noam Chomsky's writings on propaganda, say, are productive for your analysis of *Richard III*. You can certainly justify using one thinker, Chomsky, as a frame for considering the work of another, Shakespeare. But you might equally decide to shift away from the anachronistic term "propaganda" to more historically accurate terminology. Using the *OED* you might notice that the origin of the term is from the verb "to propagate." So you could examine forms the propagation (reproduction, multiplication, expansion) of information in the play. Or you might turn to a contemporary political theorist who seems interested in such information manipulation before the modern age of propaganda: Machiavelli. What term does he use for misleading or wooing an audience? He writes in *The Prince* of rulership, "nor is genius or fortune altogether necessary to attain to it, but rather a happy shrewdness." This phrase "happy shrewdness" might provide a lens for your investigations, helping you generate an organizational structure both out of the play itself, and out of historical readings connected to this play.

Writing topics

This section offers you three prompts. These range from ones we've already considered—how to write a paper structured around a particular word—to ones that might draw on your skills as a creative writer, artist, or filmmaker. My goal here is to spur your thinking—and writing. One way of approaching these prompts: lightly, with a sense of fun. Get out a piece of paper and a pen (or your computer if you prefer composing there), turn your timer to ten minutes, and start. Just start writing. You can tackle one prompt at a time. You might find you have a lot more to say about one of the prompts than the other; or you might surprise yourself with what you start writing. It might cost you thirty minutes to cover these three suggested prompts below—but it might reward you with the kernel of a great paper.

Words

As we've done throughout, here I invite you to choose one line, or a keyword, or a key scene, or even an object. In a keyword assignment, your best ally will be the *Oxford English Dictionary*. It is a large reference work available in many university libraries in multi-volume hard copy, or more conveniently now online, through subscription. If your university subscribes, I recommend you use this dictionary early and often. If we look up the word "counterfeit," for example, which Buckingham uses when he reassures Richard he "can counterfeit the deep tragedian" (3.5.5) we find three options: the adjectival and noun forms, and the verb form.

Look at definitions for all three forms, even though Buckingham uses the word as a verb. Scrolling down the list of available meanings, you will see the oldest definitions of the word comes in its verb form, meaning "to imitate," or "to forge"—to make a "fraudulent imitation of." It also means, relatedly, "to make or devise (something spurious) and pass it off as genuine." It's the next definitions that most clearly relate to Buckingham: "3. to put a false or deceiving appearance upon; to disguise, falsify," a usage that is now obsolete (at least according to the *OED*, although sometimes the dictionary is inaccurate); or "4. To put on (with intent to deceive) the appearance or semblance of; to feign, pretend, simulate"; or "5. To assume the character of (a person, etc.); to pretend to be; to pass oneself off as; to personate," another obsolete usage. You'll notice that these definitions are similar, yet their differences might be important. Is Buckingham falsifying himself, or is he feigning, or is he assuming the character of someone else? Asking these questions might cause you to wonder, what is the effect of transforming himself, even temporarily? Buckingham might imagine that he assumes the role of tragic character in order to deceive the Archbishop and others. But perhaps in the process, he truly does assume this role—after all, he becomes a tragic figure, the next victim of Richard.

Counterfeit, it turns out, is an old word. Its usages are all in play before Shakespeare writes. This is not always the case. When Richard asks Buckingham if he can look "distraught and mad with terror" (prompting Buckingham's reply on counterfeiting), he uses a word, "terror," that has a range of definitions—including some that are anachronistic for Shakespeare. Terror can mean "intense fear or dread," as Shakespeare uses it; but it can also mean "the use of organized repression or extreme intimidation," a usage dated to 1800. Thus as you peruse the *OED* you'll find modern—and potentially anachronistic—meanings of words. This dictionary thus proves invaluable in getting a sense of obsolete meanings of words that would have been available in Shakespeare's day—and also learning how words might now have meanings that were not in use in 1600. You might also use Shakespeare's Words (http://www.shakespeareswords.com). This site is available to all, without subscription, so it can prove useful especially if you don't have access to the *OED*. Here you'll find how Shakespeare uses your keyword in other plays. (This information is also available through the Shakespeare Concordance [www.opensourceshakespeare.org/concordance], which will list for you all the plays that utilize your keyword.) In the case of the keyword we're exploring here, you'll see that Shakespeare uses the word "counterfeit" many times in a famous speech by Falstaff, on honor. Perhaps comparing Buckingham and Falstaff could yield fruit? Or perhaps not. You'll also find keywords defined in the site's glossary, as with counterfeit: "to copy, imitate, simulate" or to "pretend, feign, make believe." This site glosses the word in the playtext itself as well: it defines Buckingham's use of "counterfeit" as "to copy, imitate, simulate"—but here I might argue with the site's gloss. To my ears, the second definition ("to pretend, feign, make believe") is at much at stake in Buckingham's usage as the first. So the caveat is: think for yourself as you use these reference tools.

Comparisons

Richard III and *Macbeth* are often paired. Your own thinking on *Richard III* might be honed and sharpened by investigating this comparison. You might consider writing, for example, on Richard's first soliloquy and Macbeth's. How does Richard's line "I am determined to prove a villain" contrast with Macbeth's "horrid image" that doth "unfix" his hair? Or you might compare their first long soliloquies, keeping with Richard's first speech but turning to Macbeth's meditation on the consequences of murder with "If it were done when 'tis done, then 'twere well / It were done quickly." Macbeth considers the future; as Lady Macbeth says, they "feel the future in an instant." Richard instead focuses on "now."

Reading these speeches might prompt you to consider the relationship between time and murder in these plays, exploring how conscience enters through meditation on the future or past, rather than through "now" where Richard, at least, initially dwells.

Comparing the final moments of *Richard III* and *Macbeth* is also instructive: these plays end with a more minor character assuming the throne. Both Richmond and Malcom topple sitting kings, having invaded from a foreign country (France, England). But both characters are, of course, framed as legitimate, indeed as saviors of a struggling country demonized by a tyrant. How to compare Richmond and Malcolm? Both offer closing speeches that might appear wooden in comparison to speeches by the play's heroes. If these plays could be read as morality tales, about the horror of treason, why end both plays with such uncharismatic characters? You might ask this question differently, particularly if you feel that Malcolm (or Richmond) is a compelling character.

Another instructive comparison comes in pairing Richard III with *Othello*'s Iago and *King Lear*'s Edmund. I think of these three characters as cut from the same cloth: all three use theater as bait, feigning loyalty while plotting a character's demise. Further, all three use props (such as a bible, or a handkerchief, or a forged letter) to accomplish their deceptive ends. Finally, all three claim an exceptional status: whether deformed, overlooked, or illegitimate, each of these characters feels somehow rejected and therefore justified in villainy. Yet these three characters are also, importantly, different. One way I think of their relation is through a comparison (remember Hitchcock) of these characters to a bomb: Richard III, at the start of Shakespeare's career, is the biggest bomb. He takes up the most space in accomplishing his ends. But as Shakespeare's career proceeds, he figures out how a character might have the same destructive impact in a more condensed form. Iago is no longer the hero of the drama, but a secondary character next to the titular hero, Othello. Edmund is even further condensed: a secondary character in the play's subplot. Consider the talent that Shakespeare develops over his career, to pack the energy of such a powerful character into a minor role, with an equivalent destructive impact.

Omissions and additions

As we've discussed, in mounting *Richard III* onstage, directors often substantially adapt and revise the Shakespeare text. Directors frequently add information from the *Henry VI* plays, for example, to the opening soliloquy (see Olivier's film version of the opening speech, available on YouTube, for an immediate example of this). But Shakespeare did not begin his own play by rehashing his earlier material. He begins with "Now." Why? Perhaps Shakespeare assumed his audience would already know this history, so he didn't need to refresh memories. Modern audiences, by contrast, might need help in recalling the Wars of the Roses. But there might be more literary, theatrical or formal reasons for opening the play as he does. Make an argument for the effects of beginning the play with this opening soliloquy, rather than with a dialogue between characters, or with a summary of events of the Wars of the Roses. Alternately, you might want to explore what cuts and additions you would make, arguing why they might be necessary for your production or for a better understanding of the play itself.

To approach the issue of omissions from a different angle— one is indebted to Laurie Maguire's volume on *Othello* in this series—would *Richard III* seem less funny if Richard did not talk to the audience so directly and so frequently, particularly in his asides? Read the play with an eye to these asides, and imagine re-writing a scene without them. In an exchange with his nephew, for example, Richard offers several asides, saying "[*aside*] So wise so young, they say, do never live long" (3.1.79); Prince Edward responds, "What say you, uncle?" (80), provoking Richard's formulaic answer, followed by another aside: "I say, without characters fame lives long. / [*aside*] Thus, like the formal Vice, Iniquity, / I moralize two meanings in one word" (81–3). How would the scene play without those side comments? Is it the intimacy with the audience, in addressing us, that makes such asides so powerful? Or is it the wit and intelligence contained within them? You might begin to answer these questions by noting that the short passage cited above features a noticeable contrast between Richard's speech to his nephew and his asides. He speaks to his nephew in formulaic snippets of moral instruction. But his first side comment, which offers the sinister rhyme of "young" and "long," is not an instructive but instead threatening truism—his use of "they say" is both pointed and sinister. Richard's aside on the Vice also tips his hand as a master of his theatrical craft, aware of the tradition that inscribes him. We hear the contrast between the affable uncle and the brilliant schemer in these tiny asides, making these lines do important work in establishing his character's complexity.

Analyze one such moment of audience address at the end of Act 1, Scene 1. Imagine cutting the following short lines of commentary, offered as a soliloquy after Clarence's departure and often delivered directly to the audience: "Go, tread the path that thou shalt ne'er return; / Simple, plain Clarence, I do love thee so / That I will shortly send thy soul to heaven" (1.1.117–19). Are these lines crucial to how we view Richard? What would be the effect of cutting them? More broadly, analyze Richard based on his dialogue with other characters, as if Shakespeare never included asides or soliloquies. What do you find?

BIBLIOGRAPHY

Adelman, Janet. *Suffocating Mothers: Fantasies of Maternal Origin in Shakespeare's Plays*. New York: Routledge, 1992.

Al-Bassam, Sulayman, director. *Richard III: An Arab Tragedy*. Royal Shakespeare Company. 2007.

Al-Bassam, Sulayman. "Description of the play." Available from: http://www.sabab.org/richard-iii-an-arab-tragedy/

Al-Bassam, Sulayman. [Interview by Gabriel Gbadamosi]. *Night Waves*, BBC Radio 3, broadcast 9 May 2006.

Al-Bassam, Sulayman. *The Arab Shakespeare Trilogy*, ed. Graham Holderness. London: Bloomsbury, 2014.

Aristotle. *Poetics*, trans. S.H. Butcher. Available from: http://classics.mit.edu/Aristotle/poetics.2.2.html

Bacon, Francis. "Of Deformity" (1612), in *Essays: Moral, Economical, and Political*. London: J. Johnson, 1807.

Bartels, Emily C. "Review: Shakespeare to the People." *Performing Arts Journal* 19.1 (Jan 1997): 58–60.

Becket, Andrew. *Shakespeare's Himself Again: Or, The Language of the Poet Asserted*. Vol 1. London: A. J. Valpy, 1815.

Bogdanovich, Peter. Interview with Alfred Hitchcock. 1963.

Boose, Lynda E. and Richard Burt. *Shakespeare the Movie: Popularising the Plays on Film, TV and Video*. London: Routledge, 1997.

Brown, Jeffrey. "Interview with Sulayman Al-Bassam about *Richard III: An Arab Tragedy*." Newshour (February 24, 2009).

Burnett, Mark Thornton. *Constructing "Monsters" in Shakespearean Drama and Early Modern Culture*. Basingstoke, UK: Palgrave Macmillan, 2002.

Bushnell, Rebecca. *Tragedy of Tyrants: Political Thought and Theatre in the English Renaissance*. Ithaca, NY: Cornell University Press, 1990.

Carlson, Marvin and Margaret Litvin with Joy Arab, eds. *Four Arab Hamlet Plays*. New York: TCG for the Martin E. Segal Theatre Center, CUNY, 2016.

Carroll, William C. "'The Form of Law': Ritual and Succession in *Richard III*." In *True Rites and Maimed Rites: Ritual and Anti-Ritual in Shakespeare and His Age*, eds Linda Woodbridge and Edward Berry, 203–19. Urbana: University of Illinois Press, 1992.

Carson, Rob. "The King's Three Bodies: Resistance Theory and *Richard III*." In *Staged Transgression in Shakespeare's England*, eds Rory Loughnane and Edel Semple, 79–88. London: Palgrave Macmillan, 2013.

Casey, Jim. "'Richard's Himself Again': The Body of Richard III on Stage and Screen." In *Shakespeare and the Middle Ages: Essays on the Performance and Adaptation of the Plays with Medieval Sources or Settings*, eds Martha W. Driver and Sid Ray, 27–48. Jefferson, NC: McFarland and Company, 2009.

Cerasaro, Pat. "InDepth Interviews, with Kevin Spacey," *Broadway World*, May 1, 2014. Available from: http://www. broadwayworld.com/article/InDepth-InterView-Exclusive-Kevin-Spacey-Talks-New-RICHARD-III-Documentary-NOW-Plus-HOUSE-OF-CARDS-Future-Musical-More-20140501

Charnes, Linda. *Notorious Identity: Materializing the Subject in Shakespeare*. Cambridge, MA: Harvard University Press, 1993.

Colley, Scott. *Richard's Himself Again: A Stage History of Richard III*. Westport, CT: Greenwood Press, 1992.

Cordery, Richard. "Duke Humphrey in Parts I and 2 of *Henry VI*, and Buckingham in *Richard III*." In *Players of Shakespeare 6: Essays in the Performance of Shakespeare's History Plays*, ed. Robert Smallwood, 184–197. Cambridge: Cambridge University Press, 2004.

Day, Gillian. *Shakespeare at Stratford: King Richard III*. London: Thomson Learning, 2002.

Deleuze, Gilles. *Difference and Repetition*. Trans. Paul Patton. New York: Columbia University Press, 1994.

Donaldson, Peter S. "Cinema and the Kingdom of Death: Loncraine's 'Richard III.'" *Shakespeare Quarterly* 53.2 (Summer 2002): 241–59.

Downie, Penny. "Queen Margaret in *Henry VI* and *Richard III*." In *Players of Shakespeare 3: Further essays in Shakespeare performance by the players with the Royal Shakespeare Company*, eds Russell Jackson and Robert Smallwood, 114–39. Cambridge: Cambridge University Press, 1994.

Duffy, Carol Ann. "Richard." 2015.

Erne, Lukas. *Shakespeare and the Book Trade*. Cambridge: Cambridge University Press, 2013.

Erne, Lukas. *Shakespeare as a Literary Dramatist*. Cambridge: Cambridge University Press, 2003.

Freud, Sigmund. "Some Character-Types met with in Psycho-Analytic work." In *The Standard Edition of the Complete Psychological Works of Sigmund Freud, Volume XIV (1914–1916): On the History of the Psycho-Analytic Movement, Papers on Metapsychology and Other Works*. London: Hogarth Press, 1964: 309–333.

Frisch, Morton J. "Shakespeare's Richard III and the Soul of the Tyrant." *Interpretation* 20.3 (Spring 1993): 275–84.

Garber, Marjorie. *Shakespeare's Ghost Writers: Literature as Uncanny Causality*. New York: Routledge, 1987.

Girard, René. "Hamlet's Dull Revenge." *Stanford Literary Review* 1 (Fall 1984): 159–200.

Goodman, Henry. "King Richard III." In *Players of Shakespeare 6: Essays in the Performance of Shakespeare's History Plays*, ed. Robert Smallwood, 198–218. Cambridge: Cambridge University Press, 2004.

Greenblatt, Stephen. "Shakespeare Explains the 2016 Election." Sunday Review. *The New York Times*, October 8, 2016.

Greenblatt, Stephen. "Preface to the Japanese translation of *Renaissance Self-Fashioning*." In *Shakespeare and the Japanese Stage*, eds Takashi Sasayama, J. R. Mulryne, and Margaret Shewring. Cambridge: Cambridge University Press, 1998.

Hankey, Julie, ed. *Richard III: Plays in Performance*. London: Junction Books, 1981.

Hill, Thomas. *The Contemplation of Mankinde, contayning a singuler discourse after the Art of Phisiognomie*. London, 1571.

Hitchcock, Alfred. Masters of Cinema (Complete Interview). 1972.

Hobgood, Allison P. "Teeth Before Eyes: Impairment and Invisibility in Shakespeare's *Richard III*." In *Disability, Health, and Happiness in the Shakespearean Body*, ed. Sujata Iyengar, 23–40. New York: Routledge, 2014.

Hodgdon, Barbara. "Replicating Richard: Body Doubles, Body Politics." *Theatre Journal* 50.2 (May 1998): 207–25.

Hodgdon, Barbara. *The End Crowns All: Closure and Contradiction in Shakespeare's History*. Princeton, NJ: Princeton University Press, 1991.

Holderness, Graham. "Sulayman Al-Bassam's *An Arab Tragedy:* Introduction," July 25, 2013 on MIT Global Shakespeares. [Originally published in 2007 as "From Summit to Tragedy: Sulayman Al-Bassam's *Richard III* and Political Theatre".]

Holderness, Graham. "From Summit to Tragedy: Sulayman Al-Bassam's *Richard III* and Political Theatre." *Critical Survey* 19.3 (2007): 124–43. [Reprinted in 2013 as "Sulayman Al-Bassam's *An Arab Tragedy:* Introduction."]

Holderness, Graham and Bryan Loughrey. "Arabesque: Shakespeare and Globalisation." In *Globalization and its Discontents: Writing the Global Culture*, ed. Stan Smith, 24–46. Cambridge: D.S. Brewer, 2006.

Holinshed, Raphael. *Chronicles of England, Scotland and Ireland, volume 1*. London: Johnson et al., 1807. (Original published in 1577.)

Huang, Alexander and Elizabeth Rivlin. *Shakespeare and the Ethics of Appropriation*. Basingstoke: Palgrave, 2014.

Jackson, Russell and Robert Smallwood, eds. *Players of Shakespeare 3: Further essays in Shakespeare performance by the players with the Royal Shakespeare Company*. Cambridge: Cambridge University Press, 1994.

Kazak, Fayez. "A Tale of Two Richards: Terry Grimley meets Sulayman Al-Bassam and talks to Michael Boys about Two Contrasting Takes on *Richard III*." *Birmingham Post*, February 2, 2007.

Kennedy, Dennis, ed. *Foreign Shakespeare*. Cambridge: Cambridge University Press, 1993.

Kostihova, Marcela. "Richard Recast." In *Renaissance Disability in a Postcommunist Culture. In Recovering Disability in Early Modern England*, eds. Allison Hobgood and David Houston, 136–49. Columbus: Ohio State University Press, 2013.

Lee, Adele. "'Put[ing] on Some *Other* Shape': *Richard III* as an Arab V.I.P." In *Richard III: A Critical Reader*, ed. Annaliese Connolly, 155–78. London: Bloomsbury, 2013.

Lemon, Rebecca. "Tyranny and the state of exception in Shakespeare's *Richard III*." In *Richard III: A Critical Guide*, ed. Annaliese Connolly, 111–28. London: Bloomsbury, 2013.

Lemon, Rebecca. "Shakespeare and Law." In *Oxford Guide to Shakespeare*, ed. Arthur Kinney, 548–64. Oxford: Oxford University Press, 2011.

Lesser, Anton. "Richard of Gloucester in *Henry VI* and *Richard III*." In *Players of Shakespeare 3: Further essays in Shakespeare performance by the players with the Royal Shakespeare Company*, eds Russell Jackson and Robert Smallwood, 140–59. Cambridge: Cambridge University Press, 1994.

Lindfors, Bernth. *Ira Aldridge: Performing Shakespeare in Europe, 1852–1855*. London: Boydell and Brewer, 2013.

Litvin, Margaret. "Review: Richard III: An Arab Tragedy." *Shakespeare Bulletin* 25.4 (Winter 2007): 85–91.

Lopez, Jeremy. "Time and Talk in *Richard III*, I.iv." *Studies in English Literature 1500–1900* 45.2 (Spring 2005): 299–314.

Magnusson, Lynne. "Grammatical Theatricality in *Richard III*: Schoolroom Queens and Godly Optatives." *Shakespeare Quarterly* 64.1 (2013): 32–43.

Maguire, Laurie E. *Shakespearean Suspect Texts: The "Bad" Quartos and Their Context*. Cambridge University Press, 1996.

Manningham, John. *Diary*. British Library Harleian MS 5353.

Marche, Stephen. "Mocking Dead Bones: Historical Memory and the Theater of the Dead in *Richard III*." *Comparative Drama* 37.1 (Spring 2003): 37–75.

Marlowe, Sam. *The Times*, February 15, 2007.

Maus, Katharine Eisaman. *Inwardness and Theater in the English Renaissance*. Chicago and London: University of Chicago Press, 1995.

McDonald, Russ. "Richard III and the Tropes of Treachery." *Philological Quarterly* 68.4 (Fall 1989): 465–84.

Mendes, Sam and Kevin Spacey. Program notes on *Now* website. Available from: http://www.kevinspacey.com/nowthefilm/

Mitchell, David T. and Sharon L. Snyder. *Narrative Prosthesis: Disability and the Dependencies of Discourse*. Ann Arbor: University of Michigan Press, 2000.

Mitchell, David T. and Sharon L. Snyder. *Cultural Locations of Disability*. Chicago: University of Chicago Press, 2006.

More, Thomas. *The History of Richard III* (c.1515).

Moulton, Ian Frederick. "'A Monster Great Deformed': The Unruly Masculinity of Richard III." *Shakespeare Quarterly* 47.3 (Fall 1996): 251–68.

Munday, Anthony. *A Second and Third Blast against Playes and Theatres* (1580).

Myers, Nick. "Figures of the Tyrant: The Context to Shakespeare's *Richard III*." *Société d'études anglo-américaines des XVIIe et XVIIIe siècles* 49 (1999): 25–40.

Nabokov, Vladimir. "Russian Writers, Censors, and Readers." In *Lectures on Russian Literature*. New York: Harcourt Brace Jovanovich/Bruccoli Clark, 1981.

Nardizzi, Vin. "Disability Figures in Shakespeare." In *The Oxford Handbook of Shakespeare and Embodiment: Gender, Sexuality, and Race*, ed. Valerie Traub, 455–67. Oxford: Oxford University Press, 2016.

Osborne, Charles. "How to deform King Richard." *Daily Telegraph*, July 27, 1990, p. 16.

Packard, Bethany. "Richard III's Baby Teeth." *Renaissance Drama* 41. 1/2 (Fall 2013): 107–29.

Patterson, James, ed. *Thriller*. Ontario, Canada: MIRA Books, 2006.

Pearlman, Elihu. *William Shakespeare: The History Plays*. Twayne's English Author Series. New York: Twayne, 1992.

Rabkin, Norman. *Shakespeare and the Problem of Meaning*. Chicago: University of Chicago Press, 1981.

Rackin, Phyllis. *Stages of History: Shakespeare's English Chronicles*. Cornell University Press, 1990.

"Richard III: Shakespearean Actors Rake Over the Remains," interviews by Melissa Denes, Laura Barnett, and Andrew Dickson. *Guardian*, February 4, 2013. Available from: https://www.theguardian.com/stage/2013/feb/04/shakespearean-actors-richard-iii-remains

Richmond, Hugh M. *King Richard III*. *Shakespeare in Performance*. Manchester: Manchester University Press, 1989.

Roach, Joseph R. *The Player's Passion: Studies in the Science of Acting*. Newark: University of Delaware Press, 1985.

Rogers, Jami. "The "'Fascism and Its Consequences' Season: Richard Eyre's *Richard III* and Its Historical Moment." *Shakespeare Bulletin* 30.2 (Summer 2012): 99–117.

Salamon, Linda Bradley. "'Looking for Richard' in history: Postmodern villainy in *Richard III* and *Scarface*." *Journal of Popular Film & Television* 28.2 (Summer 2000): 54–63.

Schwyzer, Philip. *Shakespeare and the Remains of Richard III*. Oxford: Oxford University Press, 2013.

Shakespeare Theatre Company. *First Folio: Teacher Curriculum Guide*.

Sher, Anthony. *The Year of the King: An Actor's Diary and Sketchbook*. London: Limelight Press, 2006. (Originally published in 1987.)

Siemon, James R., ed. *King Richard III: The Arden Shakespeare*. London: Arden Shakespeare, 2009.

Slotkin, Joel Elliot. "Sinister Aesthetics in Shakespeare's *Richard III*." *JEMCS* 7.1 (2007): 5–32.

Smallwood, Robert, ed. *Players of Shakespeare 6: Essays in the Performance of Shakespeare's History Plays*. Cambridge: Cambridge University Press, 2004.

Smallwood, Robert, ed. *Players of Shakespeare 4: Further essays in Shakespeare performance by the players with the Royal Shakespeare Company*. Cambridge: Cambridge University Press, 1998.

Snyder, Sharon. "Unfixing disability." In *Bodies in Commotion: Disability and Performance*, eds Carrie Sandahl and Philip Auslander. Ann Arbor, MI: University of Michigan Press, 2005.

Spivack, Bernard. *Shakespeare and the Allegory of Evil: The History of a Metaphor in Relation to his Major Villains*. New York: Columbia University Press, 1958.

Stubbes, Phillip. *Anatomy of Abuses*. London, 1583.

Targoff, Ramie. "'Dirty' Amens: Devotion, Applause, and Consent in *Richard III*." *Renaissance Drama*, New Series, 31 (2002): 61–84.

Tey, Josephine. *The Daughter of Time*. London: Arrow Books, 1997. (Originally published in 1951.)

"Theater Talk: 'Kevin Spacey on Richard III.'" [TV Interview by Michael Riedel and Susan Haskins]. January 13, 2012.

Torrey, Michael. "'The plain devil and dissembling looks': Ambivalent Physiognomy and Shakespeare's *Richard III*." *ELR* 30 (2000): 123–53.

Troughton, David. "Richard III." In *Players of Shakespeare 4: Further essays in Shakespeare performance by the players with the Royal Shakespeare Company*, ed. Robert Smallwood, 71–100. Cambridge: Cambridge University Press, 1998.

Urkowitz, Steven. "Reconsidering the Relationship of Quarto and Folio Texts of *Richard III*." *English Literary Renaissance* 16 (1986): 442–66.

Van Elk, Martine. "'Determined to Prove a Villain': Criticism, Pedagogy, and *Richard III*." *College Literature* 34.4 (Fall 2007): 1–22.

Walker, Elsie. "The Body of Richard and the Afterlife of Shakespeare." *Literature/Film Quarterly* 42.2 (2014): 410–13.

Weimann, Robert and Douglas Bruster. *Shakespeare and the Power of Performance: Stage and Page in the Elizabethan Theatre.* Cambridge: Cambridge University Press, 2008.

Wheeler, Richard P. "History, Character, and Conscience in *Richard III*." *Comparative Drama* 5.4 (Winter 1971–2): 301–21.

Williams, Katherine Schaap. "Enabling Richard: The Rhetoric of Disability in *Richard III*." *Disability Studies Quarterly* 29.4 (2009). Available from: http://www.dsq-sds.org/article/view/997/1181

Wood, David Houston. " 'Some tardy cripple:' Timing Disability in *Richard III*." In *Richard III: A Critical Guide*, ed. Annaliese Connolly, 129–54. London: Bloomsbury, 2013.

Films/television

Looking for Richard. Dir. Al Pacino. Perf. Al Pacino, Winona Ryder, Alec Baldwin, and Kevin Spacey. 20th Century Fox, 1996. [Film].

Now: In the Wings on a World Stage. Dir. Jeremy Whelehan. Perf. Kevin Spacey, Sam Mendes. Treetops Production Co. 2014. [Film]. The film's official website with commentary and digital scrapbooks: https://www.kevinspacey.com/nowthefilm/

Richard III. Dir. Richard Loncraine. Perf. Ian McKellen, Annette Benning, Robert Downey, Jr. Mayfair Entertainment, 1995. [Film].

Richard III: An Arab V.I.P. Dir. Tim Langford and Shakir Abal. Perf. Sulayman Al-Bassam. 2010.

Richard III: The King in the Car Park. Channel 4. Darlow Smithson Productions, 2013. [Documentary].

Scarface. Screenplay by Oliver Stone. Perf. Al Pacino, Michelle Pfeiffer. Universal Pictures, 1983. [Film].

Secrets of the Dead: Resurrecting Richard III. PBS. Darlow Smithson Productions, 2014. [Documentary].

The Hollow Crown, Season 2, Episode 3. Dir. Dominic Cooke. Perf. Benedict Cumberbatch, Judi Dench. BBC, 2016. [Television].